Mechanics Of Online Reputation Management

Repair & Control Your Name or Brand Reputation Online

By Tyler Collins

www.ORMBook.com

Printed in the United States of America
Printed by CreateSpace, Charleston SC
Available from Amazon.com and other book stores.
Available on Kindle and other devices.
First Printing, 2016

Tyler Collins
Swell Marketing, Inc
16400 Pacific Coast Hwy, #217
Huntington Beach, CA 92649
www.swellmarketing.com

ISBN-13: 978-1519762252
ISBN-10: 1519762259

Contents

V

- Dedication -

To my father Sean Collins...
For pioneering algorithms in wave science,
legendary contributions to surf forecasting mechanics,
and demonstrating the power of great reputation.

Thanks for always making the call.
Rest in passionate preeminence.

Rep-u-ta-tion:

The beliefs or opinions that are generally held about someone or something.

A widespread belief that someone or something has a particular habit or characteristic.

Introduction

Name, character, repute, standing, stature, status, position, rank, fame, renown, esteem, eminence, prestige, image, stock, credit – no matter what we call it, the nature of "reputations" have been around as long as humans have forged relationships.

Relationships with people. Relationships with things.

We are social beings. We share knowledge. We research, communicate, consume, and communicate again. Together, we learn. We learn from our own experiences, and the experiences of others. Our social instincts dictate future decisions based on what we learn through collective knowledge.

We have a community approach to our existence. Our survival depends on it. Information sharing gives rise to an abundance of advantages in our quality of life, reduces risk, and promotes safety.

We are hard wired for informational reciprocity, and we gravitate towards the most efficient means of gathering new information. Why? Every person has hundreds of decisions to make on a daily basis. Many of our day-to-day choices are habits – choices we have become so comfortable with they become second nature, requiring little, if any thought.

New decisions require thought, and to facilitate convenience in our thought process, we seek the most readily available information or feedback from our environment, and our peers.

Today, the Internet provides the quickest access to information. Community powered content on any topic. Socially infused data and perspective about anyone, and anything. With the click of a button, we access our world.

Our Digital World

Anyone with an Internet connection can emphatically agree on the fact that today's digital landscape facilitates the most efficient and convenient sharing of information in human history.

The Internet is a success. The original purpose of the World Wide Web was information sharing. Today, the primary use of the Internet holds true to that originating intent.

With the major motivation behind early digital inventions being resource sharing, it was inevitable that users (people) would find opportunities to post their opinions, experiences, and beliefs about people and things publicly. It is no surprise that people and businesses are scrambling to control what is being said about them online.

Search engines were invented to organize the world's information and media. Their primary purpose is to answer questions. People are accustomed to using search engines to acquire new information, get answers to questions, and seek new resources, products, or services.

Billions of searches take place every day for information, products, businesses, and people. Users initiate searches from desktop computers, tablets, smart phones, even televisions.

Search engine results pages (SERP's) contain a variety of types of content. Editorial and news articles, polls and opinions, business and product reviews, all these forms of information have been available online for a long time. It wasn't until search engines like Google became effective at serving these types of content to users through a methodology referred to as "Universal Search" that these opinions and reviews became more prominent in search results.

Universal Search is a methodology of displaying search content, answering to a concept that suggests users searching for a brand, product, or person, are likely interested in a variety of different media types and sources – under this approach, search engines display a variety of content (regular sites, blogs, news, images, videos, social & review sites, etc) for any given search.

The evolution of this methodology used by search engines has resulted in just about every business and individual's search results showing a variety of different resources; Some favorable, and not so favorable.

According to search engines, displaying a combination of positive, neutral, and negative content, improves the quality of the web, and the user's experience in the search engine. This position of neutrality by search engines does not always fair well for businesses, or individuals.

Why This Book Exists

Throughout this work you will encounter a smattering of validating reasons this book is important for businesses and people. Paramount to all valuations, it is designed to fulfill the promise of giving back power and control to individuals and businesses seeking to influence their digital presence and reputation online.

Every day, negative search results ruin careers, families, and friendships. They impede business growth, present unforeseen liabilities, and make otherwise normal professional relationships difficult. Negative content can destroy employment opportunities, and has the cunning ability to haunt individuals in ways that leave people feeling powerless, hopeless, frustrated, and tormented by the radically ambiguous, seemingly impossible landscape of digital search.

In order for any individual or business to recreate their reputation in online search, it is vital to possess a deep and thorough education around how search engines work, and the mechanics involved in precisely what is required to influence search results. Search optimization and online reputation management can be broken down into a science, and this book provides a surgical approach to cleansing and controlling exactly what displays for any given search query.

Both businesses and individuals need online reputation management. Often, a business unknowingly suffers from online reputation problems. Sometimes, individuals experience the same. Always is there an opportunity for every person and business benefit from a better online reputation.

Most online reputation management services and recommended repair solutions available today are insufficient for effectively eliminating negative results and producing the desired outcome in search. Among the players in the reputation management industry, there is a lack of true knowledge and experience, and a general lack of integrity when it comes to making promises about outcomes. Outcomes that people and businesses are willing to spend good money to achieve. Outcomes that can dramatically impact the course of history for a person or company.

This book is different. It covers a plethora of well-researched, battle-tested scientific truths about online reputations, search engines, and the weight certain actions have on the online reputation environment. We will shine a bright, reality-checking light on the problems and opportunities, with plenty of actionable instructions to re-imagine and re-create any entity's digital footprint.

Finally, this book exists for the purpose of knowledge sharing. If knowledge is power, then the secreting or hoarding of knowledge may be an act of tyranny camouflaged as humility. Inversely, generosity is its own form of power. What you do not know you cannot use, and the information contained in this book, formulated carefully throughout over a decade of testing and implementation, instantly becomes more powerful the moment you have it, and use it.

"We cannot solve our problems with the same level of thinking we used when we created them" – Albert Einstein

Science Over Theory

While there may be a smidgeon of theoretical perspective shared in an occasional food-for-thought context, the educational approach provided throughout this text is heavily grounded in research, application of scientific testing, and the measuring of results.

Supporting research includes years of carefully studying mind-bending organic search patents filed by Google, Bing, and Yahoo, many of which are cited in the References section, along with academic papers, agency white-papers, and various industry reports on search technology and trends. Of course, reading patents and scholarly papers only exposes one to the probable methodologies search engines use to index, score, rank, and display results, so everything included in this book has been validated through relentless testing.

"The theory that can absorb the greatest number of facts, and persist in doing so, generation after generation, through all the changes of opinion and detail, is the one that must rule all observation" – Adam Smith

As our fellow Scottish moral philosopher and economist suggests, a theory must withstand generations of validation and testing. Once it does, it may take the form of observational law.

While this book imposes no laws or rules on people and how they conduct themselves in today's Internet world, nor does it forecast or predict what comes on the far horizon with search engines, it does provide factual evidence of effective strategies for repairing an online reputation, with a strong consideration for the historical evolution of search engines, the current methods they use, and Internet user behavior. Evidence supporting the importance of a positive online reputation will be provided, along with a thorough explanation of possible strategies for successful management.

Theory is worth its weight in facts. Let's agree to focus on facts.

What This Book Is Not

Any business' reputation begins with its operational mindset, and its actions or non-actions can result in its customers either posting something positive or negative online. Many books have been written on the best practices for product development, customer relations, and business operations, but very little information exists around how to clean up a bad reputation, negative editorial, or unfavorable content online.

Although some of the material covered in this book could be considered "guerrilla tactics" for market domination, digital penetration, branding hacks, or social manipulation, we will not be covering much traditional marketing, branding, public relations, customer relations, or business operations best practices.

That said, approaching this process with an education and some experience in the application of traditional best practices can be of great benefit. Those concepts and tactics for business growth and management are not without their value, and continue to serve business and individuals around the world

For those that would consider this book incomplete without them, there is a section towards the end that does cover some of those concepts. But again, there are plenty of books dedicated to those topics and the purpose of this one is to empower the reader in ways the others simply cannot.

Furthermore, this is not a book that treads lightly around ethics, or potentially unsafe conduct. Without reservation, we expose strategies and tactics used by the most elite reputation management experts, with transparency and perspective on the options, risks, liabilities, impact, and viability of each.

Internet User Behavior & Search Trends

Internet user behavior evolves as rapidly as new sources of information and platforms for engagement become available.

For individuals, this means that every month, week, or day there might be a new website to submit a product review, a new blog to read about their favorite topic, or a new social platform on which they have to create a profile in order to be where their friends are. New sources for information research appear, with new forums for voicing opinions, resulting in more data, everywhere, about everything, for everyone to consume. As users engage, they develop relationships with digital entities and pave reputations throughout communities.

For businesses, this means that they have to regularly adapt digital marketing strategy, engage in new advertising, publish more content, establish a new presence on the next rave business profile site or social platform, and constantly adjust business operations to the current yet always changing standard of having the right information and media in the right places to achieve the right digital presence. As users find more ways to post, comment, share, and review, the stakes for businesses rise as their presence evolves. This also means that they may unknowingly have a business "presence" somewhere without actively creating one. Remembering our social nature, people are going to share their experiences with a product or company with or without the business' consent.

Search engines, however, provide a refreshing consistency for both individuals and businesses. Although the nature of the content available on search engines constantly changes, there's general consistency in the types of content, and in the platform itself. People search, read, analyze, and click. Here exists a series of reliable control variables for people and businesses, which (among other reasons) are why there are not many search engines that people use today. A few search engine companies play the game well and the trust and convenience they provide keeps them in the game.

However, the nature and "intent" of user searches has evolved, and will continue to. For a long time most consumers would simply search for whatever it was they wanted to find, learn, or buy. "Cheap Flights" "Desktop Computer" "Women's Shoes" "How To Make Mint Ice Cream" etc.

With the growth of consumer review sites and trends with social influence, people began searching for a "brand-name + reviews", or a "product-name + reviews", or even the creators or executives behind them, such as "brand + CEO". Nowadays, people are accustomed to checking the validity of an information source, a business, or a person behind a company, and the results they see strongly influence their decisions as a consumer.

Today, over 80% of Internet users begin their session with a search engine, which makes sense because every mobile, tablet and smart device sold today is preinstalled with either Google or Bing by default.

- 3 Billion searches per day, amounting to over 1 Trillion searches per year, take place on Google alone.

- 55% of those searches are conducted by users with an "intent to buy" something.

- 97% of people research a products, services, and brands before making a purchase.

- 77% of search engine users never click past the first page of search results.

It is safe to conclude that the results displayed on the first page of the search engine make up the majority of a business or personal online reputation.

Online Reputation Impact

With a few strokes of the keyboard, individuals can post their opinions about a business, product or person online, and there are dozens of big, authoritative website platforms that exist specifically for this purpose. The reason this is important is because the size, age, strength, and trust these mega sites maintain plays a huge role in the reputation management process. In later chapters, the weight these review sites have in the scope of reputation management will become clear, but what makes a positive online presence so necessary today?

Impact On Individuals

Individuals are often caught up in swells of editorial, news, and review content pushed to the web. Whether it's the personal name of a CEO running a company who is highlighted in some form of online content publication, specific details of a person's personal lifestyle featured in a rogue blogger's endeavor to expose behavior or share opinion, or a falling out of professional stature – there are hundreds of events that might lead to someone's personal name being featured in negative online content.

For a person, a digital reputation can begin as early as high school or middle school. These days, many tech-savvy children publish rich media content to the web on a daily basis, spending countless hours on social platforms like Facebook, Twitter, Instagram, YouTube, Vine, and any other name-the-trendy-platform community where their friends are. Lunch break clicks, campus behavior, and extracurricular student events give birth to rumors, gossip, and offline reputations that frequently take form in the digital world. Sure enough, if the comments or opinions are published online, search engines crawl and index the pages they are on and before an unsuspecting child knows it, there they are featured like a tarnished celebrity in some take-down editorial column at the top of the search engine. Parents are often shocked to learn that their child has an online reputation problem before they ever seek a job interview.

Adults experience escalated personal name reputation liabilities and opportunities online. Whether interviewing for a new job, working for an existing employer, seeking a partner for a business opportunity or life, the content served for a person's name search has weight and impact on the circumstances, opportunities, and outcomes in their current and future life.

Arrest records and mug shots, court appearances, marriage disputes, unethical professional practices, or employer/employee misconduct all have their place online. Individuals are often shocked to learn that the local government keeps records of their residents in their digital database, or that the employer they worked for committed some unforeseeable act that became associated with their personal name while they worked at the company, or that a former coworker they were involved with decided to embark on an Internet crusade and is now blogging about their affair together. These types of situations are rarely expected to become visible to the public, yet every day hundreds if not thousands of people realize they have negative content about them on the first page of the search engine.

Even as early as 2010, a study by Microsoft and Cross-Tab Market Research revealed that 70% of companies have rejected candidates based on the candidates online reputation, but only 7% of Americans believe it affects their job search. While a survey by CareerBuilder.com found that 1 in 4 hiring managers used search engines to screen candidates. One in 10 also checked candidates' profiles on social networking sites such as Facebook.

Impact On Businesses

The shifts in search demand dictate that users are often best satisfied by socially infused content, giving merit to the concept that suggests a positive online reputation is important for businesses today. Users expect to find a community driven collection of information about a business, product, or service for any given search query. And even if they do not expect it, they usually get it.

With a strong majority of consumer buying decisions being dependent on whether or not they can locate and validate reviews or opinions about the product or service they are considering for purchase, the importance of having a positive online presence should be apparent to businesses.

In today's search engine landscape, it is not uncommon for review related editorial content to appear at the top of results for a company's brand-name search, even if the user does not include a search modifier that indicates they are seeking review content. Most businesses today focus only on their singular website, which in reality, can only secure one or a few of the results on the first page of the search engine. This leaves the remainder of the typical ten results open for the search engines to decide (based on mathematical calculations) what content best serves the user, and if the search engines operate with a mentality that seeks to provide users a variety of content, there is a high probability of editorial or review content being present in the top results.

When a user searches a business or product name and they see additional resources or consumer review sites available for them to access, they naturally gravitate towards those sources (at least with a mental note to revisit and check later) even if they click on the primary business website source first.

Negative reviews, unfavorable news stories, employee profiles, customer uploaded images, or blog articles all have the influential power of derailing a business' growth. Detrimental and horrifying complications can arise for companies that have negative content present in the search engines. Of course, search demand varies by industry sector, and some organizations are searched for more than others, but rarely is there a business that would not benefit from a better online search reputation.

Don't Be An Ostrich

Similar to many problems people face in life and business, the obstacles and liabilities presented by negative online content often remain undiscovered, undervalued, and unresolved by the people under the wrath of impact.

For those acting under the assumption nothing is wrong or causing interference with life or business in the digital search space, it is recommended to do some mild due diligence in order to confirm or invalidate what may or may not be visible to other interested parties through a simple search engine query.

For businesses, the statistics around Internet user behavior should be enough to convince a business owner of the importance of having a positive online reputation. Either way, there are perspectives to consider.

1) If a business' online presence is an important component to its growth strategy, then managing its online presence is vital. Statistics prove that a strong majority of any business' potential or existing customers or clients will research that business. The results that show influence their decisions and are easier to control if approached before it gets bad.

2) If a business has not yet analyzed their brand name in search, and has yet to thoroughly analyze the positive and negative content that is being displayed, they should. If the situation appears OK, one should know that at any moment it could become bad. Additionally, if the situation is already bad, its not the end of the world – there is help available and this guide provides numerous methods by which someone can suppress negative content, and repair the results with positive assets that support business growth.

Who Cares

Although multiple examples have been provided which highlight the potential advantages and disadvantages of positive and negative online reputations, it is worth mentioning a few additional relationships that an online reputation could positively or negatively influence.

Consumers

Any person or organization that uses economic services or commodities is a viable candidate of someone whose decisions are occasionally, if not regularly influenced by digital information.

Business Partners

Alliances between multiple parties in business formation have been around for centuries. Securing appropriate partnership relationships can be risky, and people in business are typically well researched and diligent about their decisions. In many cases, sourcing and establishing business partnerships can be a vital component to a successful venture, where two or more entities join forces to compliment each other. Behind these decisions to create alliances are people. People who use search engines to learn about the people they are considering for a partnership venture.

Stockholders

Investing in the ownership of public or private stock in a corporation warrants calculated investigation and decision making about the viability of a prospective business investment opportunity. Shareholders are typically curious, analytical individuals with no shortage of resources to make educated decisions about where to invest or keep their money. Search engines provide a quick and efficient way for stockholders and investors to source information about an organization, product, or an individual before making an investment decision.

Marketers

Professional marketers understand the value of leaving an impression in the public eye. As it is with many in the employment sector, a marketing professional might choose not to contract their services to an organization or individual with an abundance of negative content online in a desire to steer clear of what promises to be an uphill battle in reshaping the reputation at hand. The marketer might also devalue the opportunity if he or she has a limited understanding of how search engines function or the technical aspects of digital content. Alternatively, a marketer may use an obviously negative online reputation as a means to secure that same opportunity with the promise of repairing it. The point is, the marketer cares. Or at least, should.

Journalists

Publicists and editors have an uncanny ability to uncover stories, curate, extrapolate, manufacture SPIN, and produce or leverage negative press for attention. Gathering, processing, and disseminating news to an audience is what they do. With or without a professional position, journalists typically have a satiating appetite for newsworthy content. In our current digital world, both the primary tasks and output of journalists are being executed and consumed on the Internet. Combine this with abundant opportunities for publishing on well-trafficked, search engine friendly content platforms, editorial and news content consistently proves to be among the most commonly problematic sources of negative information that invoke the need for online reputation repair.

Employers

Business owners and hiring managers read cover letters, resumes and applications, and check references before making final hiring decisions. Depending on the employer and the nature of the job, employers often search candidate names in search engines to learn more about the person they are considering for the job or contract. Online research of job applicants is becoming a common practice, if not a standard operational guideline, for many businesses offering employment opportunities. The presence of negative content about a prospective job candidate in the search results consistently serves as a safeguard for businesses navigating the risks involved in making the right hiring choices for their organization. Additionally, some employers will choose one candidate over another if one person's online presence seems stronger and facilitates the positive impression the applicant intends to make on the employer.

There are many examples of how certain individuals lend merit or attach value to another person's online reputation. Whether they are professional or personal, co-workers, associates, friends or family members, our social-inspired digital society has a governing stronghold on our lives today.

You Care

Above all others, the person who probably cares the most is you. If you do not, of course that is your choice. However, whether or not you assign value to your online reputation and image, you do have an important life. Your life has value and so do the relationships and things you care about. Whether or not you enjoy it, despise it, or accept it, your life is impacted by the online world. To gain a greater knowledge of how you can access, influence, control, and leverage digital content for greater advantages, continue throughout this book. As you do, you will discover that your reputation, as seen through the lens of the World Wide Web, is ultimately something you are empowered to create, consistently re-imagine, and direct.

History Of Reputation Management

Before The Name

For some career experts in search engine optimization and digital marketing, online reputation management has been a practice since before it was called online reputation management. Impacting top positions in search with a website or content property for a given search query is the fundamental goal of any SEO (search engine optimization) strategy. A special few of the more visionary practitioners have always aimed to control an entire search vertical, because they know that the more results they control on the first and second page of the search results, the more visibility, influence, and authority they have in the marketplace.

Crises Evolution

Socially influenced content visibility propelled by the rapid development of voicing platforms for any person with an Internet connection has significantly accelerated the problems that surround businesses and individuals in need of online reputation management.

Collaborative studies between analytics groups have determined some interesting statistics:

♦ 86% of online U.S. adults have used a search engine like Google to find more information about another person.

♦ 75% of online U.S. adults have searched their own name in a search engine. Of those that searched their own name, almost half (48%) said most of the search results about them are not positive; nearly a third

(30%) said nothing shows up about them at all.

- Nearly a third (31%) of online U.S. adults that have searched another person online have looked up a politician. Of those that did, over half said the search influenced their voting decision.

- Among online U.S. adults that have searched someone else online, 42% have searched someone before doing business with them. Of those that did, 45% have found something that made them decide not to do business.

- Almost half (43%) of online U.S. adults that have searched someone else online have searched a potential date, significant other, or ex-boyfriend/girlfriend, making romantic searches one of the most common search among U.S. adults.

Rise of Demand

Naturally, people who use search engines regularly entertain their curious desire to search their name or brand name in the search engine. Business owners and executives started catching on first, realizing that the content referencing their business in search results could have a positive or negative impact on their brand. Upon discovering content and media with a negative sentiment, businesses and executives began seeking solutions to repair and control search results. Individuals followed suit as they discovered they could do the same for their personal name.

Services

Following demand, reputation management service options gained traction and became available to people and organizations. Services range from content removal campaigns, positive consumer review strategies and solicitation, search engine optimization, negative property suppression, branding and rebranding, and many slices of proactive and preventative measures designed to cleanse, repair, polish, and dictate what appears in search engines, on news sites, and across business and professional profiles and review sites.

From DIY (do it yourself) options to high price done for you options, individuals and businesses today can choose from a plethora of reputation management strategies. One of the purposes of this book is to help the reader navigate those choices and become educated about the nature of reputation management problems, intelligently investigate the available services, and make educated decisions around the most viable strategies for their given situation.

To quickly access reliable reputation management services, hop to the "Done For You Services" section at the end.

Reputation Concepts

Reputation Attacks

Reputations in general, are vulnerable to digital attacks and many types of attacks are possible. An attack is, by its very nature indicative of malicious intent, wherein the attacker actively seeks to cause damage to a person, business, or entity by creating any form of negative or unfavorable content that becomes visible to the public.

Attackers can be journalists, bloggers, consumers, competitor businesses, or anyone seeking to damage another entity by way of digital content. An attacker may also be considered to be anyone publishing content that is damaging, with or without malicious intent. This can involve many basic or highly sophisticated forms of attack, from publishing one article or review to the mass creation of pseudonymous entities to gain a disproportionately large influence.

Public Relations

Press releases, news stories, and media editorials have powerful influence on public opinion and perception. Press can serve as an originating source of a reputation problem, and it can serve as part of a solution. Without monitoring and management, a business and in some cases individuals, can be negatively impacted by online press content. With proactive strategies in public media relations, press and journalism can prove to be a fortifying channel for positive online reputations.

The most skilled reputation experts leverage the power of the press by tapping into the publishing power journalists have on trusted news platforms, along with utilizing SPIN tactics and self-publishing options to submit press releases to authoritative websites in order to promote a positive brand presence and suppress negative content. However, throughout this book it will become clear that simply publishing a press release to the Internet is rarely enough to produce the ultimate desired outcome.

Online Reviews

Very few businesses with an online presence are without some form of publicly visible consumer reviews, which often encourages the need for review strategies that aim to organically or artificially generate positive user reviews about their business, services or products. Organic strategies may consist of proactive customer relations and outreach programs to existing customers, soliciting feedback and comments on the business' public review profile.

Artificial solutions often involve the singular or bulk purchasing of reviews wherein the business can customize what is said in the review, along with any other criteria such as star ratings or the platform on which the review should be posted. While review strategies can sometimes shift consumer impressions and increase overall star ratings, it is important to note that focusing only on reviews management usually results in only a partially fixed reputation situation.

Social Media Management (SMM)

Properly managing audience communications and sentiment on social platforms is often a vital component to ensuring an entity's positive online presence. Without monitoring and management, a social profile can become a serious reputation liability. Internet users frequent the social media profiles of businesses they transact with, and the presence of user generated negative comments, unwanted posts, and unsupportive reviews on a business' profile can turn what was once a community asset into a rampant, sometimes viral environment that decreases brand loyalty and impedes business growth.

If having a social media presence is a choice or an important component for a business' success, then having a proactive social media management strategy is crucial – however positive social media is rarely enough to completely control a business' or individual's online reputation.

Search Engine Optimization (SEO)

Search optimization is the process of influencing top positions in the search engines by optimizing <u>and promoting</u> websites, content, and other forms of media. In reputation management, the SEO component is designed to infiltrate search results with chosen media content, for the purpose of suppressing negative material that the person or business wants to eliminate.

SEO is, or at least should be the central focus of an online reputation management strategy. A reputation repair campaign that does not heavily focus on search optimization is going to fall drastically short of creating the desired result. The assumption is that the individual or business is convinced that the content displaying on the first (and maybe the second) page of the search engine is importance for public impression.

Understanding all the factors involved in controlling an entire first page of search results, and having the resources and means to execute on that knowledge is vital. However, even most of the SEO and reputation management service companies today have a limited knowledge of the science, and are lacking the resources to be effective, or are not willing to invest in the time, energy, and technology required to achieve the results for their clients.

For any given search query there are hundreds of ranking factors and variables being calculated simultaneously in order to sort and deliver the set of results a user sees. The tactical strategies in this book cover search engine ranking factors in great depth and provide realistic perspectives and instructional resources for achieving the necessary outcomes.

Content Removal

In some cases, it is possible to get negative content removed from a website. Usually, this requires a legal letter from an attorney representing the compromised party, or communication with the owner or webmaster of the site in question.

Successfully removing negative editorial, reviews, or blog posts are a rare accomplishment in the reputation industry, but it can be done depending on the circumstances. Although these special occasions do exist, one should not expect a successful outcome and base their entire reputation strategy around the hope that content can be successfully removed. The unlikely probability that content will be removed or deleted speaks to the importance of other strategies, such as suppression campaigns through search engine optimization.

A strong majority of content cannot be removed by someone who does not own the website it is on, therefore it is important for the person seeking reputation management to consider all forms of solutions for optimizing the name search vertical

DMCA Removals – The US Digital Millennium Copyright Act criminalizes production and dissemination of technology, devices, or services intended to circumvent measures (commonly know as digital rights management or DRM) that control the access to copyrighted works. In the event a copyright, trademark, or other protected intellectual property has been infringed, a "Demand" may be filed with LumenDatabase.org, which sends takedown requests to Google.

Spam Bots

The Internet is very much like a playground for marketers and programmers with an inclination towards gray area tactics and market manipulation, and many types of automation tools exist for simulating tasks and events online. Everyone is familiar with the concept of computer viruses, wherein a software program infects the host computer or web server and performs certain actions, usually with malicious intent to access, inject, or extract information.

Spam, unsolicited marketing messages, user communications, profile creations, content posts, and website attacks are all things that can be automated through Internet software. Spam bots may be used for mass injections of comments on websites or denial-of-service (DOS) attacks on website servers in an effort to force websites to shut down. These tactics are commonly referred to as "black hat" methods, which can do harm to website owners and typically do not add value or safety to the Internet.

Negative SEO

Search engine optimization is most appropriately considered a positive, growth-centric practice that leads to increased placement in the search engines, however the search engines employ thresholds that detect when someone is using too many optimizations on or external to the target website property. These thresholds are designed to prevent SEO specialists from gaming the search engine results and help to prevent low quality, untrustworthy content from achieving top placements.

 Experienced SEO experts understand where the lines are drawn with website optimizations, and some have the ability to exploit these thresholds in ways that results in a web property moving backwards, or down in the search results. Most people have a misinterpretation of what negative SEO is and how it's done, and as a result, most who attempt this method fail.

Astroturfing

Canvassing third-party websites with fake and artificial reviews, comments, and content with anonymous accounts is sometimes referred to as astroturfing. Many just call this spam. The term astroturfing (rarely if ever used in the industry) is a derivation of "AstroTurf", a brand of synthetic carpeting designed to look like natural grass, and a play on the word "grassroots". The implication behind the term being that there are no true or natural roots, but rather fake and artificial. Some may consider this concept and practice a useful component to a strategy, but it rarely sustains any long-term or meaningful impact.

Marketing

Brand marketing strategies are typically focused on communicating the value of a product, service, or brand to customers for the purpose of further promoting or selling that product, service, or brand. A strong marketing campaign executed in the right way, at the right time, can thwart the damaging effects of a negative online reputation for a brand. Many forms of digital marketing prove to be useful in preventing and repairing negative reputations, but they can also lead to damaging an online reputation.

If a company's operational conduct or product quality falls short of promises made in marketing messages to consumers, it can lead to backlash in the form of negative reviews and editorial. A good example of this is in the nutritional space.

Frequently, we see situations where companies craft messaging to consumers with the promise of gluten-free or non-GMO consumables, resulting in the Food and Drug Administration releasing enforcement reports online that warn the public of health concerns. Like clockwork, nutritional bloggers and journalists begin blanketing the web with their disdain for the brand's dishonest claims.

Blunders aside, well engineered marketing consistently proves to be a reinforcing asset in a digital reputation campaign and should be a core component to any business that values its online presence as a growth strategy.

Streisand Effect

Occasionally, attempts to hide, remove, or censor a piece of information has the unintended consequence of publicizing the information more widely. This phenomenon is referred to as the "Streisand Effect", named after the American entertainer Barbra Streisand, whose 2003 attempt to suppress photographs of her residence inadvertently drew further public attention.

Similar actions resulting in this effect can include cease-and-desist letters, public statements, appeal procedures, and any action that draws more attention on the negative or unwanted information.

Pursuing solutions without a thorough investigation of unforeseen outcomes can result in more detrimental outcomes than existed with the original problematic source or information. Reputation repair should be thought of as a tactical mission to swiftly control or eliminate negative content online.

Ethics

As stated in a previous section, this is not a book that aims to tread lightly around ethical best practices, or crusade with raised flags for right and wrong. Think of this book as a consultative resource that sides with no particular tactic as the best solution, but allows the reader to make educated decisions around the best options for a given situation.

The individual or business seeking help or clarity may or may not be concerned with ethical boundaries, so this section exists as a means of providing perspective and potential justification for the tactical options available.

Causes & Effects (Perspective)

Reputation problems arise from as many unique scenarios and circumstances as there are people and business with the need for reputation repair. Usually, reputation problems originate from an event relating to misconduct or distrust, socially unacceptable behavior, or objectionable practices by an entity, so it's important for every person and business to consider reshaping and adhering to their fundamental operating values and decisions.

Additionally, there are circumstances where the person or business did nothing wrong or harmful to anyone or any particular organization, yet they are negatively impacted by online editorial or reviews that may or may not be true information or an accurate reflection of the situation.

Take for example a company offering an exercise program for weight loss that produces results for those who do the exercises, but produces no results for those who do not do the program correctly. The people who do not implement the program correctly then go online and write negative reviews about the program, saying that it is a fraudulent scam, sending other potential candidates for the program away from the offer.

Another example might be an online commerce storefront that clearly states an "all sales are final, no refund" policy on purchases from their website, yet when consumers realize they cannot return their product for a refund they post negative comments about the company, claiming the company is run by thieves that stole the shopper's money.

In medical practices, doctors who perform procedures on patients know that they must disclose risks to patients, yet it is not uncommon for the patient who encounters one of the fully disclosed risky outcomes of a procedure to go online and produce a blog about the doctor, suggesting they engaged in malpractice.

Outside the professional sector, individuals often become associated with another party's conduct or behavior. For example, a publicly recognized executive at a financial firm becomes featured in a New York Times article about a lawsuit and government intervention on the firm because a partner at that firm committed tax fraud, and that executive now has that story associated with his personal name for life – even though he had no direct knowledge or involvement in the tax evasion or events leading to the lawsuit.

The wife of the uninvolved executive in the above fraud case now has her name associated with that story because the editor at the New York Times used a picture featuring the husband executive and the wife at a dinner party, with a caption saying *"husband-name right, wife-name left"*. This wife is a 2nd grade school teacher, now facing the loss of her teaching license because her husband's partner in business committed tax fraud.

While these situations are all uniquely qualified for further consideration and justification, there are hundreds of similar circumstances like these that become a reality for people everyday.

State of Emergency

People and organizations suffering from negative online reputations are often in a state of emergency, and some could be considered a state of danger. Individuals facing job interviews are afraid that their potential future employer is going to Google search their name (sometimes a recent high school or college graduate). Businesses operating with integrity are scratching and clawing towards any sign of hope and profit, but are plagued by the one negative article that appears in the top position of search, and will likely go out of business as a result.

Negative search content can act as a ball and chain, a social and professional prison, a lifestyle and business handicap, and a psychological stressor that can catastrophically debilitate a person's ability to function properly in life.

Risk & Liability

The Internet serves as an automatic liability for any business and individual. Conversely, there is equal opportunity to engage in solutions for improvement and gain. Though it may not seem that way for those currently impacted from negative exposure, the reality is that the Internet is an equal playing field – it simply depends on how intelligently and aggressively one approaches the game.

In coming chapters, many liability scenarios and problems are explained in detail. For those considering reputation management services and strategies, it might be worth considering some risks surrounding proactive action and passive non-action.

Considering the typical state of emergency and burning desire people experience when facing a reputation problem, many are compelled to contract any company promising to provide a solution, or any strategy that seems to be effective in theory. As stated earlier, not all companies offering solutions today are properly positioned to provide effective or sustainable solutions, and many of them make an already bad situation worse. In fact, most so-called "reputation management companies" are not even companies, they are resellers of other agency services – agencies over which the resellers have no influence or control.

Reputation management services today often fall short of even the most fundamental best practices around website development, content marketing, news publishing, social media management, and search engine optimization. Frequently, a business or person contracts a firm for "reputation repair" and ends up with poorly written articles, unprofessional social profiles, low quality images, and unfavorable video content and embarrassing website properties showing up in the search results. Making it worse, the client wasted money and the negative content or review site that was the focus of the campaign is still positioned at the top of the search engine, maybe higher and more prominently visible than before the campaign started.

The receiver of reputation management services may be misled or unaware of tactics used by the firm they contracted for services. Many reputation management companies mass-post artificial content or use automated software programs to attack open website portals as a primary function of their strategy, framing their efforts with buzzwords like "content marketing" and "press release strategies". Efforts like this may lead to further tarnishing of an entities reputation as they face the aftermath of negligence by the firm.

Inversely, the firm's services may actually produce quality digital content, press releases, and useful media, but the reputation organization's experience begins and ends with editorial efforts and has no true capabilities in achieving top placements in the search engines with the quality content they produce.

As many horrifying circumstances that exist in the reputation management service industry, there are a few great companies that perform amazing work. SwellMarketing.com has a 100% success rate in online reputation management campaigns (See "Done For You Services"). This book also serves as an effective guide to navigate an industry full of misperception and risk.

Passive non-action is an option, but at what cost? A typical wrong assumption by people needing reputation solutions is that not many people are seeing the negative content. This is rarely the case, and there are usually more sources of negative content visible than are readily observed.

Justification

Statistics of Internet user behavior and a thorough valuation of a positive online presence may serve as a means to justify a business' or individual's need for online reputation management. Situational severity varies wildly depending on the nature of the searched name, along with the type, sentiment, and volume of content visible in search results. Due to the rambunctious variety of situations and circumstances that lead to reputation problems, and the robust palette of management solution choices, casting a standardized ethical blanket on the entire industry could be considered morally reckless.

People with a strong adherence to normative ethics and moral standards may find the following principles helpful in a case-by-case approach to justifying reputation management tactics. Arriving at a short list of representative normative principles is itself a challenging task. The principles selected must not be too narrowly focused, such as a version of act-egoism that might focus only on an action's short-term benefit, and those on opposing sides of an ethical issue must see the principles as having merit. For this reason, principles that appeal to duty to God are not cited since this would have no impact on a nonbeliever engaged in the debate. The following principles are the ones that seem most appropriate for ethical discussion around reputation management:

Personal Benefit: acknowledge the extent to which an action produces beneficial consequences for the individuals in question.

Consequentialists would agree that moral discourse should be determined solely by the positive and negative outcomes from a reputation management strategy. Although there are layers of consideration involved in consequentialism, the general concept suggests that if the total good consequences outweigh the bad outcomes, then the action could be considered morally right. If the bad consequences were greater, then the action would be considered morally improper.

Social Benefit: acknowledge the extent to which an action produces beneficial consequences for society.

A properly executed reputation management strategy may produce quality, useful, informative content for Internet users. Conversely, it may suppress content that serves Internet users with sufficient warnings and risk assessments necessary for healthy decisions.

Principle of Benevolence: help those in need.

Reputation management companies tend to use this exclusively as a means to justify selling someone reputation management services, regardless of their misconduct or the nature of the reputation problem.

Principle of Paternalism: assist others in pursuing their best interests when they cannot do so themselves.

Reputation management may serve as a means to more effectively help people access a product or service offered by a company, or may assist a professional or person move on with their business of life. Reputation management companies may use this as a means to justify providing services to an individual or company in need of help.

Principle of Harm: do not harm others.

Measuring the potential harm to others as a byproduct of reputation management may be a difficult experiment to accurately calculate. Assessments of public impact and safety may be a concern, along with any damage or harm possible to websites involved with the contracted firm's tactics.

Principle of Honesty: do not deceive others.

It is not uncommon for clients of reputation management services to have little to work with in terms of "positive" content to share or promote. By the very nature of lifestyle and business practices, many prospects are lacking in the areas of newsworthy or blog-worthy material. As a result, the fabrication of information is a common practice by reputation management firms as they "reach" for facts in their efforts to produce new content assets.

Principle of Lawfulness: do not violate the law.

Very few legal lines are clearly drawn on the battlefield of digital marketing and Internet conduct. Things like Copyrights, Trademarks, and Hacking are obvious red lights on the road to success, but people often cruise through these intersections without even knowing it. With or without clarified legal guidelines for web-based actions, the relationships between client and contractor often materialize into the greater risk.

Principle of Autonomy: acknowledge a person's freedom over his/her actions or physical body.

Like doctors performing surgery on a patient, or a contractor renovating a home, service providers may choose to honor a client's choices for the sake of capitalism. Under a different spin, a reputation service provider may apply an abnormal ethical hard line and honor the freedom of speech rights for users or journalists providing the negative reviews and editorial (highly unlikely).

Principle of Justice: acknowledge a person's right to due process, fair compensation for harm done, and fair distribution of benefits.

People suffering from reputation problems are often good people operating under a respectable code of conduct and have been unfairly attached to a problem. Like criminal attorneys and corporate litigators striking deals with opposing counsel and judges on behalf of their clients, reputation experts may choose to defend anyone who seeks their help.

Rights: acknowledge a person's rights to life, information, privacy, free expression, and safety.

Enough said.

Search Scenarios & Problems

The following sections highlight obvious and not-so-obvious events and circumstances that either directly or indirectly generate reputation problems for people and businesses.

Industry Perceptions

Product and service type vertical markets and certain industries in general sometimes give rise to skepticism or collective misunderstanding about the nature of the products and services available. Beyond an individual entity's reputation, industries themselves can acquire a bad reputation that leads to difficulty in marketing and growth for businesses trying to operate under that particular market umbrella.

Bad News Coverage

Negative news and editorial content amount to a significant percentage of reputation problems in today's society. Journalists, editors and media agencies have the ability to publish stories and announcements about anyone, and any business, covering any one of the scenarios listed here.

Certain topics are more likely to receive news coverage than others, but any entity and circumstance featured in the news automatically receives an increased amount of visibility.

News sites typically sustain large audiences and readership retention. Combine that with strong domain authority and the trust media websites maintain with search engines, any published content on these sites gains traction and top placement quickly.

Lawsuits & Legal Documents

From FBI investigations and FDA enforcement reports, to disbarred lawyers and criminal convictions, lawsuits and related legal documents have their place in digital content publishing.

Many of the regulatory and enforcement filings that have publication consistency are the automatic output from system generated document sharing and filing processes used by local and national government IT infrastructures. Others are the manual archiving and sharing by officials at various organizations and associations.

Mug Shots & Images

Digital photo publishing, archiving, and sharing frequently result in unfavorable images appearing in both regular web search and image search results.

Many different events and circumstances result in unwanted visible images, and dozens of Internet platforms exist specifically for sharing image content. Some of these sites, like the ones with millions of arrest mug shots, are engineered to scrape and republish public record databases.

Arrest Records

Similar to mug shots and image platforms, many websites have been developed to source and republish court case filings and arrest records.

Engineers behind the more sophisticated versions of these platforms incorporate advanced technology that curates the gathered content for the reproduction of unique profiles on people and businesses, which the search engines respond to positively with prominent placement for related searches.

Scam & Ripoff Reports

Anyone can create and publish a scam or ripoff report on anyone or any business. Websites like ripoffreport.com and scamgroup.com are among the dozens of platforms that allow any person to publicly announce fraudulent allegations in a rich content format.

The search engines grant these scam report websites priority in search results and neither the sites nor search engines perform much, if any, due diligence on the people filing the complaints or the content being published.

Consumer Review Sites

Business and product consumer reviews are now an expected form of information across the landscape of online commerce. Kids, parents, business owners, and professionals, literally anyone with the ability to purchase a product or subscribe to a service can provide a review based on their experience.

Online consumer reviews have become a standard in our digital society and there are hundreds of different website platforms in existence with the sole purpose of ingesting and rendering these user generated reviews to the public.

Competitor Attacks

Since the dawn of capitalism (before it was a concept actually) businesses have endured a competitive landscape. The Internet with all the options for publishing and the widespread visibility of content is a supercharged medium for competition, and attacks on competitors. Attacks materialize in the form of fake reviews, negative press, dispassionate blog posts, manipulated images, even hacking and assaults on website servers.

Trademark & Copyright Infringement

Unlawful use of trademarked names, service marked images, and copyrights can result in multiple types of reputation problems. The case where an ethical or unethical business infringes on a competitor name or logo can become a news story or lawsuit which compromises the infringing party, while the infringed business or owner of the legally protected content suffers from public confusion and reductions in brand loyalty.

Fraud & Scandals

Tax evasion, money laundering, extortion, hedge fund fraud, foreclosure and bankruptcy fraud, lottery scams, homeowner and senior citizen fraud, and any type of socially or legally objectionable scandal will quickly find its place into online editorial and scam report platforms. The bigger the crime, the larger the announcement, and broader the impact.

Hate Sites

Organized groups advocating hatred, hostility, or violence towards members of race, ethnicity, nation, religion, gender, gender identity and sexual orientation, or any other designated sector of society often have independently owned and operated websites dedicated to the publishing of opinions and content. Members or advocates of these groups often cloak themselves as anonymous users on other sites where they promote animosity, hostility, and malice against a person or entity.

Cyber Squatting

Also known as domain or name squatting, the registering, trafficking, and/or use of other entity names are a common tactic of people endeavoring to profit from the goodwill of a name or trademark belonging to someone else. Domain names, user accounts, and other properties can be purchased, secured, or controlled by another non-authentic party, who then may use the property or account to exploit or extort the authentic party.

Doppelgangers

Commonly referred to as look-alikes and doubles, it is not uncommon for a person or public figure to have a doppelganger. In some instances, doppelganger images and behavior can cause reputation problems for a person or public figure. Doppelganger images are frequently manufactured with graphic design programs and further promoted to gain visibility and attention. Many celebrities are so unfortunate to have doppelgangers of them in the pornography industry, taking the form of image and video content.

Job Changes

Seemingly less newsworthy, job and career changes and the reasons behind them can materialize into editorial news or content. Employment termination, conspiracy theories, and reallocations of human resources are sometimes featured in the media, causing problems for both individuals and businesses. Additionally, the employing company may feature a newly hired employee in a press release, causing a variety of unexpected personal and professional challenges for the person.

Name Changes

As it is with home ownership, marriage, business filings, and court cases, name changes are included in public record. Information in the public record, by its very nature, is available to the public. Many Internet websites exist for the sharing of public record information.

False Information

Invalid fake information can be manufactured by any person for any reason, and there are thousands of website platforms and tactics a person can use to publish or share information that may not be grounded in factual reality. Both people and businesses experience the impact of false information about them on the Internet.

Fake Profiles

Websites that offer social communities and personal or business profile options are a double-edged sword. Even though the larger platforms are becoming better at verifying the identities of user accounts, it is not a perfect science and most websites do not.

Fake profiles are created every day, sometimes in bulk, for the purpose of spamming, mass posting, or the sharing information for gain or profit, and these efforts can have compromising effects on people and businesses.

Rogue Bloggers

Privately owned websites with blogging features and public blog platforms offer aspiring writers opportunities to flex their journalistic muscles. Its not uncommon for businesses and individuals to realize a blogger has seemingly made it their mission in life to slander and defame them through a series of blog posts.

Blogging platforms are typically search engine friendly by default and some webmasters know how to make sure blog content achieves top placement and visibility for a brand, product, or person related search query.

Ex-Employee Slander

People excuse themselves from employment or face termination from jobs for thousands of reasons, and many ex-employees feel empowered by taking their opinions and experiences public.

Similar to consumer review sites, job and employee review websites are ready to intake and display an employee's experiences and reviews of the former company they worked for. Emotionally charged by their departure, many employees can perform serious damage to a former employer.

Industries, individuals, and unique entities are subject to online reputation damage resulting from any of the many possible events and scenarios explained above.

Typical Problem (or Opportunity) Websites

Reputation problems originate from a variety of predictable sources for a common set of reasons, and there is commonality in the types of websites that contain the content that typically transpires into something problematic.

The typical websites that produce troubling negative content are important to understand and analyze from a search optimization perspective, because the only way to combat the effects of these sites have on an entity's reputation is to formulate a strategy that speaks to the type, format, intent, and authority these sites possess.

The same websites that cause reputation problems can also be powerful assets in the repair process. Only by fully understanding the purpose and influence of these problem websites can one successfully use the same websites as a component to a positive reputation strategy.

In later chapters this book covers in detail exactly how to exploit such opportunities, however be advised with an early disclaimer: Posting content to these websites is rarely, if ever enough to produce a positive result in itself. There are dozens, if not hundreds of necessary factors to consider in successfully utilizing these websites for reputation improvement.

News

Moving through many different forms of media, news and editorial content is essentially packaged information about current events or industries. Most printed news agencies, local and national in nature, use a web-based platform for publishing. Some news organizations are centered on strictly digital formats of content. Online news information is such a massively distributed and consumed type of content that search engines like Google and Bing have created search features dedicated to serving news content under an exclusive interface. Search engines display news related content under regular web search results.

The articles and stories are often weighted with strong importance and positioned with prominence due to the authority of the news websites on which the content originates. Due to the trust news websites inherit from reader audiences and therefore search engines, news websites are a leading source of reputation management problems. Alternatively, a brand or person with a public relations strategy can leverage the power of news websites to gain top placement in search results with a favorable story or article.

Editorial

Any document or page written on a topic and based on opinion, with or without affiliation to the featured topic, is considered editorial content. Editorial websites range from News sites, Blogs, Content Sites, Product Review sites, and many other forms of opinion-driven content publishing platforms where individual pages and articles exist on a topic, industry, event, place, person, business, or trend. Industry specific editorial sites can be of great value in a reputation management strategy, along with having the potential to cause great problems for an entity if the opinion of the literature is not fueled by positive sentiment.

Blogs

Individual and multi-author informational sites consisting of discrete entries ("posts") allow writers to deliver a scheduled or unscheduled series of chronological article features to the public on any topic. Blogs are often viewed as a channel of free speech, allowing writers to weigh in with their opinions, research, announcements, and insights on any pre-defined or ambiguous set of topics. Blog features may be deployed on privately owned websites, public content platforms, government sites, and university sites (ie: student blogs). Due to the limited restrictions on blogs and the authors producing content for them, blog related content often surfaces in search results about a business or person, and can become either a liability or be used as a positive asset in reputation management.

Forums

Internet forums, or message boards, are online discussion sites where people hold conversations in the form of posted messages or "threads". Forums can be general purpose or topic specific in nature. Messages can be a concise comment, question or a longer write-up on an area of focus or problem, which are often organized under specific topics of interest. Forum users are allowed to comment and collaborate in threads with other people, sometimes resulting in long web pages full of people's comments, opinions, praise, or complaints.

Forum pages (usually individual topics or threads) are indexed by search engines and often gain traction in the search results quickly. In reputation management, a forum thread is not usually a reliable asset in a repair campaign and more commonly pose as a liability, due to the free speech nature of the platform and participating users in the forum.

Video Sites

Many websites offer video hosting and publishing options, and some are exclusively designed for the archiving and publishing of user's video clips or productions. Popular video platforms such as YouTube and Vimeo are extremely authoritative with the search engines, with millions of users constantly engaging in the publishing, viewing, and sharing of video content.

Users of video platforms are offered a variety of engagement options from uploading and publishing video content viewable to the public, as well as creating video channels, organizing playlists, liking or disliking specific videos, or leaving comments on other people's content. Users, channels, playlists, and unique videos all receive a uniquely defined page on the video platform that search engines analyze, index, and serve in the search results. Videos and pages on these platforms allow for advanced optimization techniques such as titling, describing, tagging, even the polishing of video transcripts and captions – all of which are viewable and readable by search engines.

Search engines treat video content with special consideration, as they are a unique form of media content that provide unique value to users searching on various topics. Like other content publishing platforms, video hosting websites offer users an element of free speech and behavioral expression, amounting to a wide range of videos featuring any imaginable topic, born from all points in the spectrum of opinion and sentiment. Videos about people and business often show up in top positions in search, sometimes as a positive or negative review or opinion about the company or person, which can lead to reputation problems or opportunities.

Scam Reports

Websites that feature content specifically relating to scams, fraud, and ripoff claims are typical in the landscape of reputation management problems. These websites allow anyone to claim that another entity is conducting a scam or suggest something in society is a ripoff. The most popular of these scam sites are commonly referred to as scams themselves, because many attempt to extort money out of the business or person featured in the submitted report, requiring them to fork over large sums of cash to even "respond" to a report published about them.

Many a frustrated business owner is baffled by the mob-like mentality under which these sites are allowed to operate, and often the only economic solution to combat the negative effects these sites have on a reputation is to conduct a brute force search optimization campaign to suppress the publicly visible reports displaying in search.

Government Sites

Earlier chapters reference how local and national governments archive and make public record information available to Internet users, and these sites are often a major problem for people with reputation management needs. The nature of content that can arise from a government filing such as a court case, lawsuit, intervention, legal offense record, or other matter of public record is not typically positive in nature.

The government sites themselves (with the .gov domain extension) maintain an extremely high level of trust with the search engines, and in the public eye. Any page visible to search engines can be indexed and displayed in search results, and is usually awarded a top position by default. With very few access points for regular citizens, government related sites are usually only on the problem side of a reputation situation and can rarely be used as a tool in a repair strategy.

Image Sites

Much like video hosting and publishing platforms, many websites today allow image publishing features and some are built exclusively for uploading, archiving, and organizing images and albums of images. These image platforms contain search features for discovering image media, and every discoverable image can also be found and indexed in the search results of search engines.

Search engines treat images similar to videos in that they provide a unique format of media content, which may serve to be useful in the process of providing users correct or differentiated answers to their search queries. Search engines like Google and Bing have a dedicated "Image Search" that allow users to search exclusively for images on the web. Image search results are often the source of reputation problems in both the independent image search environment as well as regular web search.

Negative image reputation problems can be difficult to overcome because of the authoritative nature of the sites on which the images exist. Search engines award tremendous authority to image platforms like Flickr, Pinterest, and others that have billions of images available for the search engines and users to access. Image websites can be both a source of problems and opportunities for improved online reputations. Later in this book we cover how to influence image search results and the precise steps to leverage opportunities using image platforms.

Review Sites

Consumer and business review sites are available in great abundance throughout the Internet. Ranging from national consumer report sites to smaller local business reviews, these review websites allow users to submit reviews on any given website, business, person, product, or service depending on the platform. Examples of review sites include Yelp, AngiesList, TrustPilot, Choice, Better Business Bureau, Google My Business, etc. Review sites are social in nature as a majority of the visible content is user-generated and provided by the public.

Comments embodying sentiment, passion and opinion can vary wildly and are often associated with a 1 to 5 star review. Typically, all comments and opinions published to reviews sites about a business or person are contained in a centralized profile page for that business or person, which search engines can read, index, and serve in their search results. Due to the nature of origin for the content contained on reviews sites, the frequency with which users access review site content, the size and authority of review sites, and unique value these types of sites provide users conducting searches, profile pages on review sites gain momentum quickly in the search results and often stick in the top positions.

Profiles on review sites can be a very positive asset in reputation management or they can be an extreme liability. The difference is how well the profile is managed and maintained by the owner and the contributions from the public on that given profile. Be cautious of relying exclusively on any profile that allows public reviews, as these pages can get out of control quickly and may be extremely difficult to transform into something positive.

Social Platforms

The phenomenon of digital social networking underwent remarkable growth after the early platforms like MySpace and Facebook were created. Along with the original big players, today there are hundreds of social networking websites like Google+, LinkedIn, Instagram, Reddit, and Twitter that allow users to build social relations among people who share similar interests, activities, backgrounds, real-life connections, or nothing at all. Individual users can create public profiles featuring details about themselves, including biography content, images, videos, employment history, interests, favorites, friends, travel agendas, and a variety of different details about themselves that they wish others to see.

Many platforms offer businesses the opportunity to create public profiles to represent their brand, product, services, or website, along with any and all details pertaining to the entity they wish to display. Most social platforms used today offer individuals and businesses posting features that allow them to make announcements, share resources, ask questions, or post anything they desire to show up in the content feeds available to users in their social network. Search engine crawlers devour these sites and receive a fire hose like influx of user-generated data, and just about anything they can read is stored in their index.

Individual and business profile pages are rich with unique content and serve as a unique type of web property that search engines will commonly display in search results about that business or person. In reputation management, a properly managed profile page on a social platform may serve as a positive asset whereas a poorly managed profile may turn into a source of negative information and problems for the entity owning the profile.

Employment Websites

Also known as "job" sites, these websites deal specifically with employment and career opportunities. Many employment websites are designed to allow employers to post open positions with job requirements for prospective candidates to apply to, and others offer employer reviews, career and job-search advice, and describe different jobs or specific employers.

Considering the user generated "reviews" features many of the bigger employment sites offer today, many employer profiles become littered with past or current disgruntled employee reviews about the company where they are currently or were formerly employed. The profiles on these job sites are readable by search engines and contain many of the rich details that search engines and users consider unique, often resulting in priority search placement for a brand.

A well-managed profile on an employment site can be a positive asset in a reputation management campaign, but could also be the source of a problem depending on the nature of the employee reviews and how well the profile is populated with helpful information.

Profile Sites

Ranging from personal-social profiles to professional and portfolio and business related profiles, many websites exist for individuals and businesses to create unique pages about themselves on public sites. Hundreds of sites are dedicated to allowing the creation of individual profile pages, and many other sites not exclusively dedicated to social networking also contain social features and profile creation options.

Almost every social networking website allows a user (whether representing themselves or a business) to create a unique profile about themselves. Other website types like News sites, Forums, Image and Video sites, and many other non-socially oriented sites also allow users to build a unique profile page about themselves. Business and people profiles show up in search results frequently for a person's or business' name search, and the content on those profiles leaves an impression with anyone who views them.

Usually rich with details and content, profile pages are often considered a unique and relevant resource. Interestingly enough most profile creation sites do not require a thorough validation step to qualify the person or business creating the profile. Even sites like Facebook allow any user to create a "Fan Page" profile under almost any name – this named profile, which now labels what could be a very optimized profile on a person, business, or topic, often quickly occupies a top result in search.

Many businesses and individuals find profiles created about themselves that did not originate from an authentic source, which can pose severe reputation problems if the profile created does not represent them in a positive light. Alternatively, a profile page can serve as a positive asset in search reputation results depending on how it is created and managed.

School Related

Academic institutions regularly insist on having a strong web presence for course and administration related information, and many offer students the opportunity to blog, publish work, organize information, or create profiles. Many academic sites (defined by the .edu domain extension) are infrequently moderated and allow public submissions of content, with many entry points for current or alumni students to publish content.

Many students find that other students have written negative things about them on a University student blog, and some teaches suffer the wrath of wide-spread student dissatisfaction and low professor ratings. Additionally, teacher review sites exist for the purpose of allowing students to share opinions and experiences about the educators they encounter throughout their academic journey. Once again, our socially dependent society takes form in the digital world in the materialization of academic reviews and editorial.

Reputation problems can originate from school related sites, and for those who monitor entry points into .edu and academic site publishing options, school related sites can serve as an asset in a reputation strategy. Later in the book we discuss how many experts acquire link citations from academic websites to further boost the authority and trust of other properties on the web.

Every day a new Internet platform is born with the potential to become a mega-publishing site. From industry specific interest groups, to local and regional community sites, to personal profiles and special interest forums, websites launch constantly allowing the public more and more ways to post, publish, create, share, comment, like, dislike, upload, archive, organize, present, communicate, collaborate, and control their relationship with the world around them.

From highly moderated news websites to open forum platforms, there are hundreds of sites that allow the sharing of rich media and information. Understanding the nature of problems and the sites on which they originate is a knowledge foundation required to properly assess reputation damage and formulate an effective strategy to successfully combat the negative affects these sites have on a reputation.

Assessing Reputation Damage

In order for one to determine a strategy that will effectively inoculate against negative search results and damaging content, or to determine if a strategy is needed, one must investigate the results across a variety of different criteria. The following set of recommendations will preface future chapters with instructions on gathering essential information needed in order to navigate the best options for reputation solutions.

Before beginning search research, know that it is not necessary to add punctuation or abbreviations or hyphens between words when searching – unless those modifiers are common attributes of the name under consideration.

Upon following the steps provided below, the person conducting the reputation research should take inventory (create a log or list) of negative results that appear and the search word combination that rendered the results. The search combination (set of words used to search) can become the focus of the reputation repair campaign.

Negative results are often easy to spot, and other times negative content can be less glaring. One should investigate each link that displays in the first two pages of search results by clicking on each link and analyzing the text content, images, and overall sentiment of the page to determine whether or not each link is positive, neutral, or negative.

Make a clear list of negative properties and pages that are not desirable, and consider the positive and neutral properties as potential assets in the reputation management strategy. The process by which one can utilize positive and neutral assets for reputation repair will be explained in future chapters.

Personal Name

Everyone should search their personal name in Google and Bing, and any search engine commonly used directly by them or their associates. The obvious first step is to search the first given name and last family name. Secondly, it is recommended to search the full name: first, middle, and last. Finally, add prefixes, suffixes, and business or professional associations, along with any possible current and past school or community affiliations.

Examples of this research might include a person's full name + college name, full name + the company name they work for, full name + association name they are a member of.

- ♦ Common Name (First + Last)
- ♦ Full Name (First + Middle + Last)
- ♦ Name + Company (First + Last + Company)
- ♦ Name + School (First + Last + School)
- ♦ Name + Organization (First + Last + Organization)

Note, the "+" is not required in order to render accurate results for the name and affiliation combinations.

Company or Brand Name

Similar to personal name research, brand or company names should be analyzed with slight variations. Beginning with the most commonly referenced versions of the company name (ie: Company Name), followed by entity abbreviations or extensions (ie: Company Name, Inc). The same research steps should be conducted for any current or past subdivision or brand subsidiary names, along with any regional modifiers relevant to the brand. For example, a cellular phone company may launch a prepaid phone brand under the parent company, or a solar panel installation company may have a sales subdivision with a specific name.

Any name or brand phrase used by a company when interfacing and communicating with the public should be investigated to determine whether or not any negative content or results appear.

Product Names

Consumers may research a brand's flagship products, new releases, version upgrades, and any product or service name used by a company in their attempt to validate trust, performance, and quality before making a buying decision. New products compel consumers to perform research. Every electronic device, clothing line, athletic product, fitness program, financial service, and consumable food product inspires consumer curiosity and leads them to research that product or service by name. Assessing reputation research for product names involves searching the product by name, by company + product name, including or excluding any common or less common abbreviations.

Employees

Hiring managers and business owners often search an applicant's name in the search engines before selecting a candidate for employment, but very few follow up with reference checking and employee name research after the person is hired. Considering that employees often interface with customers or business associates by name, the negative digital reputation of an existing employee can have a detrimental impact on a company if discovered by a prospect, existing customer, associate, or partner. This is more common with larger organizations and key executives, but many small businesses suffer from these less obvious reputation problems as well.

Business owners and managers at organizations are encouraged to investigate the online reputations of existing employees by following the personal name research recommendations as a way determine if there are any risks associated with that person's employment at the company.

Website Name

A website name is not always a direct match to a brand, company, or product name, and in reputation management research, should be treated as its own entity. People often search for a website name as opposed to the core brand or product name. This is common because people do not always remember the name of the parent company they maintain an interest in, and are revisiting a former shopping or research process based on memory.

Website names are often referenced in content publications, editorial, review sites, and scam reports. Searching the full website name, with and without the domain name extension (.com, .org, .net, etc), with and without common spacing or punctuation, will allow a business or website owner the opportunity to see the results that reference the website. Keeping in mind the usual 10 results on the first page of the search engine, the user conducting the search for the website may not always click the first result. The search for a website name often produces unexpected results below the primary, actual website result and may lead the user to a property that casts a negative impression on the person interested in the website or associated brand.

Usernames

With the rise of social media, people and brands forge identities with the public through usernames on publishing platforms, cloaking their real identity or posing as a different, fun, or recognizable name for the sake of sharing content and media. It is not uncommon for users of Instagram, Facebook, and Twitter to have hundreds, thousands or millions of followers, and the usernames associated with these accounts develop reputations. Similar to website names, usernames should be researched in the search engines to determine if any unwanted content exists.

Search Modifiers

Users of search engines often modify their searches with slight delineations in order to retrieve more accurate or relevant results. Common or possible search modifiers should be analyzed, as the search results that display from these modifiers may be wildly different from the unaltered original search query.

- ♦ **Locations** – Include the location (city, region, etc) associated. Additionally, change the search location in the search engine, to retrieve results the search engine has determine relevant for that location. This can usually be done by clicking a button at the top of the search engine interface and manually changing the location.

- ♦ **Variations** – Consider common variations of the name or brand, including prefixes, suffixes, entity or website name extensions, product names with year of release or version codes, etc.

- ♦ **Name + Reviews/Complaints** – Attach the word "reviews" or "complaints" after any name, brand, product, or website search, and analyze the results that display. This modifier will often produce a different set of consumer review sites and resources that may not contribute to a positive online reputation.

- ♦ **Autocomplete** – Search engines offer a feature that "suggests" alternative or related searches as the user types in their desired search phrase. These suggestions may prove to be useful in understanding the commonly searched variations of a brand, product, or person. Using the autocomplete suggestions to research alternative searches may be a way to uncover more opportunities to improve an entity's online reputation.

Determining Reputation Strategy

Depending on the nature of the reputation problem, a certain type of repair solution may be required to effectively cleanse and control search results. The natures of reputation problems vary, as do the strategy solutions available. The following sections highlight the most effective reputation repair solutions for the most common problems that exist today.

Controlling Search Engine Results Pages (SERP's)

Almost all online reputation problems can be addressed by some form of search engine optimization. SEO for reputation management focuses on improving search results in either regular web search or other results tabs like images and videos. Within this general concept of improving SERP's (search engine results pages), a few different approaches are possible.

Suppression

The most common and practical of all reputation management strategies, and solving the strong majority of reputation problems, suppression campaigns can be used to push negative content down in the results by pushing positive or neutral content up. This common strategy often leads to insufficient methodologies deployed by agencies and individuals attempting to control reputations, as the process by which one completely controls an entire search vertical requires an extremely high level of SEO sophistication and experience, along with robust systems and processes to achieve the result.

Suppression campaigns must involve several types of digital media content optimization, a precise type and sequence of publication and promotion, and a calculated, steady hand. A suppression campaign is an ideal solution for anyone facing search results containing negative content they cannot control, change, or get removed.

Reputation control through suppression, powered by search engine optimization, is the primary solution covered in this book as it is the most needed and most sophisticated form of online reputation management.

Image SEO

Also known as image optimization, image SEO is a strategy that specifically addresses the elimination or suppression of negative image content in either image search or images appearing in regular web search. Image SEO may be a viable strategy for anyone suffering from negative images (i.e. mugshots). Image SEO can be a powerful component to reputation control through search optimization & suppression campaigns, and is often an important piece of a brand or individual's online reputation management.

Negative SEO

The objective of negative SEO is to exploit and exceed thresholds of proper search engine optimization for a given page, or aggressively damage a website or webpage with an inbound attack on the server or means of hacking. These efforts target the negative property directly in an attempt to move it down, as opposed to focusing efforts on promoting other positive content that could move above it. As explained in the reputation concept section, negative SEO aims to exceed the known thresholds of proper website optimizations (both onsite and offsite), or attack the website in such a way that convinces the search engine it is no longer a trusted resource.

Emphasizing the word "trusted", the search engines make their own decisions about which sites are considered trusted, and which are not. Note this disclaimer: many websites that are the source of negative content are considered "white listed" with the search engines, meaning that they are essentially immune to these types of over-optimizations and attacks. That being said, someone with a decade of high-level SEO experience may still be able to exploit the ranking factor thresholds on these types of authority sites, because although certain website domains receive what could be considered a "free pass", the individual pages on these websites are not immune to certain optimization factors such as keyword density (percentages of words on the page and pointing to the page through links).

Website and specific web property type optimizations will be covered in great detail in future chapters. The big takeaway about negative SEO is that it rarely if ever works, because either the target being attacked is not a viable subject for negative SEO influence, the attacker is not experienced enough to execute the strategy properly, or the search engines translate the attackers attention to the target property as a sign of increased authority for the target page. In other words, if negative SEO does not work, it will likely result in the target property becoming stronger and ranked higher in search results.

Improving Reviews

Many circumstances warrant escalated attention to consumer and business review channels, especially if the platform and profile is of importance to the business or person. If this is the case, there are numerous ways to increase the volume, frequency, and sentiment of online reviews. The options for review optimization can vary from creating or purchasing fake or artificial reviews placed on the profile or platform by way of artificially manufactured comments by employees, friends, or ghost accounts, to the more organic generation of positive reviews through the solicitation of customer feedback.

The nature of these strategies vary and the choice to engage in these types of options is a decision the person or business owner must make by weighing the ethical concerns and benefits of the different options along with a true understanding of their customer base or audience. Fake reviews may not be a good fit for a business' code of values, yet soliciting positive reviews from customers might not be a viable option either. Depending on the importance of the profile or platform on which the negative reviews are present, a suppression campaign designed to eliminate this property from search results may be a more practical or desirable approach to combating the impact of negative reviews.

Content Removals

Removing content from the Internet is often the most desired outcome from anyone facing a reputation problem, however this happens to be the most unlikely outcome of any reputation management strategy. In order for one to get content removed from a website, they need to either be a webmaster of the website the content is on, be friends with a webmaster of the website, or have a legitimate legal angle to play that challenges the owner of the website and forces them to remove the content.

Legal approaches require lawyers and legal letters, which often require money. These "lawyers" and "legal letters" do not always have to be legitimate to get the attention or action response desired from the website owner, and many people make attempts to get content removed with what appears to be a strong legal claim against the website owner and the target content.

News sites, review sites, and any community or editorially driven content site – good luck getting content removed. The chances of successfully getting content removed are slim. Occasionally, enough complaints of violation on a YouTube video will do the trick, or several notices to Yelp about a fake business profile, but most of the time these efforts are futile. Removing content may be vital component to online reputation management given the nature and location of the information, and some experience success depending on the approach, but formulating an entire online reputation management strategy around the hope that content will be removed is likely to fall short of the overall desired outcome.

Social Media Management

Managing a social media audience may be the beginning and end of a reputation strategy, but only if the reputation problem exists exclusively on the target social media platform. With so many fantastic, personal and professional approaches to managing social media channels, this is rarely if ever the primary source of reputation problems. People complaining or commenting negatively on social media are probably doing the same in other areas of the Internet, and a person or brand's reputation usually spreads beyond just social.

However, if the reputation problem can be repaired entirely by improving the experience of the individual or organization's audience on a social platform, it is a situation that can be addressed through a strong social media marketing campaign. If a social media property is a risk to a business or person, or was artificially created and/or is outside the business or person's control, a suppression campaign may be in order to eliminate this property from search visibility.

PR Strategies

Similar to social media management, press strategies are one unique aspect of a possible reputation management strategy. There are few reputation situations that can be completely repaired by positive press, but press releases and proactive relationships with media agencies and editors can prove to be very useful in the process of improving the digital reputation of a brand or person.

Shifting public attention, creating positive content assets, and utilizing press releases as an SEO mechanism are viable options within the landscape of reputation management options. Suppression campaigns often have a strong PR component incorporated into them because press releases and news content can be a supporting force in promoting other positive content.

To recap, most online reputation problems are best resolved through search engine optimization strategies engineered to suppress negative content from public view. Suppression campaigns often incorporate several or all of the unique approaches that address specific content or platforms, and sometimes it is possible to achieve the desired result by utilizing all of those approaches simultaneously.

Due to the volume of reputation problems that call for search engine optimization and content suppression, the remainder of this book will be primarily dedicated to exploring those strategies.

Reputation Control & Search Engine Optimization

Questions, queries, phrases, words, brands, products, people, events, news, locations, records, history, instructions, tutorials, videos, images, presentations, audio, documents – all searchable and visible in search results.

Anything searched presents a combination of different visible results. Anything visible can be optimized for higher placement, or suppressed by way of optimizing and carefully promoting the results around it.

The first and second page of search results for any given brand or person are the primary make up of an online "reputation" – therefore, it is reputation management through search engine optimization that provides the most effective and sustainable means of not only repairing, but controlling reputations online.

Viability

If executed by someone with experience and sophistication, online reputation management through search engine optimization is a powerful and effective method for combating the damaging effects of unfavorable online content.

The desired outcomes and the quality of campaign results are usually in direct correlation with the experience of the executing agent responsible for the campaign. A campaign implemented by someone with little experience in SEO reputation management, or done by someone only willing or capable of deploying a partial approach, will probably not achieve the desired outcomes.

Many reputation repair services and solutions act as quick-fix band-aids, or result in unsustainable positive reputations long-term. As a science, SEO is a difficult challenge for even experienced marketers, largely because the search engines constantly adapt their ranking algorithms to the shifting digital environment in an effort to better serve their users, which leads to an evolving playing field. Most marketers and webmasters are not equipped to stay ahead of SEO changes, and encounter obstacles along the way of achieving an initial top result in search, not to mention sustaining top results achieved.

Alternatively, advanced SEO and reputation management experts that invest themselves heavily in the study, implementation, and testing within the professional science of search optimization, can achieve and sustain search engine results for individual sites or many properties in a singular search vertical.

By using strategies contained in this book, industry experts and new practitioners will have a greater chance of delivering improved or completely repaired online reputations through search engine optimization.

Nature of Control

In order to control one's reputation online, one must first master the playing field within which a reputation is derived and repeatedly forged. First, understanding the originating source of reputation problems is crucial. The source of the problem might be mindset, operational conduct, affiliations, events, a code of values, or general practice that lead to the unfavorable information being shared or posted on the Internet. Secondly, possessing technical mastery over the websites, platforms, audiences, and search engines that render and serve the negative information is vital.

Only by understanding the fundamental source of the reputation problem is it possible to avoid repeating more of the same conduct that proves to be incompatible with a positive online reputation. Only by having a deep understanding of the Internet environments in which reputation problems exist can one approach the repair process with skill and effectiveness.

The potency of control is in direct correlation to the mechanism of skill one has to determine and influence the behavior of the search engines, or the visible content on the target platform. Search engines operate with a set of rules (mathematical formulas) that govern the way information is displayed. These rules are not clearly defined for the general public, they change frequently, and only the most diligent SEO and reputation experts have the prerequisite knowledge required for even attempting such influence over search results, and the studious gumption necessary to stay in the game.

With the right knowledge, a tenacious drive for learning, the foresight to see changes on the horizon, and the wisdom to know what actions will yield a positive result, reshaping search results proves to be a powerful mechanism of reputation control for many.

Risk of Engagement

Improperly implemented SEO reputation management campaigns can result in damaged websites, worse reputations, lousy article content, lost money, more stress, handicapped quality of life, and more of the unwanted byproducts of the original reputation problem. Sometimes, "no results" is a risk itself – so it is vital to partner with a firm that has a proven track record and process with merit.

Readers are strongly advised against choosing any reputation management company that promises clean search results without a strong background in search engine optimization and a proven history of successful work in the industry. Many firms operate with outdated methodologies that do not meet current SEO standards, make wild exaggerations on the promise of success, or mislead clients into thinking the work is done for them when it is really a DIY (do it yourself) play.

The biggest risks with reputation management through search engine optimization are associated with misleading services and firms that do not operate with a code of conduct beneficial to all parties involved. These situations can result in a plethora of undesirable outcomes in the digital and offline world. More risks will be covered on a case by case basics throughout the tactical journey that lies ahead.

Opportunity

The opportunity for a positive online reputation exists for all people, and all businesses, it is simply a matter of commanding circumstances and resources that make it possible. Understandably, circumstances often dictate the need for reputation repair, so it is important to inventory those circumstances and resulting scenarios diligently. Resources follow demand, and the tactics contained in this book answer the needs of those with or without a problem, whether it is a positive reputation one wishes to dictate from a state of emergency or a situation of low-pressure imagination.

The right time for reputation attention is now. Anyone can begin the repair or control process and start taking immediate action on a better future online reputation. This is a process that requires time and attention, and there are very few, if any quick and permanent fixes.

Once a properly executed SEO reputation management campaign matures into success, it can serve as a digital firewall preventing old and new negative information from surfacing in the search results. Many successful clients of suppression campaigns refer to the reputation management process as an insurance policy against future problems, and many people and businesses are taking advantage of the opportunity to get ahead of their digital reputation needs before problems appear.

Decisions

Based on Internet user behavior statistics and the increasing dominance of our electronic lives, beginning the process of search reputation improvement seems appropriate for all people and business today. Ultimately, every reputation under consideration has a unique set of determining factors that may or may not justify following a process of repair or control.

Considering that the inevitable alternative to proactive action is less control, less influence, less dictation over personal and professional results, and less command over success in life and business, it is the author's wholehearted opinion that the process of search engine reputation management begin promptly, and without reservation.

The following chapters delve into the scientific aspects of search engine functionality and optimization, the mechanisms of control available to those seeking influence, and the precise actions that produce results. Whether or not one has made a final decision on strategy, or if reputation repair is needed, the following chapters promise to be a thorough education in search engine optimization.

Era of Universal Search

Hundreds of contributing factors (calculations) are involved when a search engine formulates sets of results to satisfy a search, and several scoring models and specific aspects of these algorithms pertain to reputation management.

In 2007, Google Inc announced what they refer to as "Universal Search" & Blended Results, which introduced content from their vertical search platforms into regular web search. Vertical search content like "images" and "videos" and "news" are now fully integrated into our normal web search results experience. Today, all of the major search engines use this integrated approach to serving results to users.

Universal search aims to integrate multiple types of media content into the results for any given search query, resulting in a more diversified set of results for the user performing the search. The introduction of different content types in regular search results is designed to show a variety of information sources in hopes that the diversification of content from regular sites, blogs, news, images, videos, social posts, documents, review sites, etc, will more accurately answer search questions and increase the user's experience in the search engine.

How Search Engines Work

For the purpose of this book and the online reputation management process, it will be useful to have a general concept of search engine technology and how they work, however in no way does this section (or book) aim to fully document the highly technical people, hardware, software, and mathematical processes with which a search engine successfully accomplishes its objectives. That is another subject worthy of its own book – or 100 books.

In a general sense, search engine companies contract scores of the most advanced software engineers, mathematicians, and information technology professionals in the world, who create eye-blurring algorithmic formulas to read/count/measure/calculate/score/rank and serve information, using campus-sized farms of computer networks and servers for automated machine learning and the intelligent organization and delivery of the world's information and media.

Primary Purpose

Search engines serve one primary objective: To correctly answer questions.

Anything searched is considered a "query", and queries are considered questions. Questions must be answered correctly, or the search engine fails at its objective. The correct answering of questions is what makes a search engine company successful. In fact, search engine companies go to great lengths to achieve a correctly answered question without forcing the user to click a result.

Today, we see answers to search queries presented on the immediate page of results. For example, search for "US President 2015" and big and bold at the top of the page is "Barack Obama" with an accompanying picture of the President. Search for "100 divided by 3" and the correctly calculated answer of "33.3333333333" is present inside a visible calculator available for the next math problem one wishes to enter.

Search engines are very good at answering questions, and one of the ways they do this so accurately is by utilizing a variety of media types for serving correct answers to queries.

The takeaway, is that search engines will consider any content type and media format they can successfully read and index, and will utilize any of those information sources and media files in their search results in an effort to provide a complete set of satisfying search results (answers!) for their users.

Indexing & Media Types

Most people think of search engines as a portal to search for websites, but search engines actually provide a lot more than typical website results. The search engines read and index many types of content and media. Website pages, blog posts, news articles, social profiles & posts, tweets, bookmarks, images, videos, document formats like .PDF and .DOC, presentations .PPT, books, products, mobile applications, flights, maps, and many other media type formats. If the media type is digital, they attempt to understand it.

A healthy approach to understanding search engines and media types is to assume that if a search engine can access or read a document, it will attempt to understand and index the document, and the more it can understand about the nature of the document or source of information/media, the better equipped the search engine is for serving that document type to its user base.

The take away, is that search engines utilize many different types of document formats and content types to better serve users with accurate search results. This becomes a vital piece of fundamental knowledge when approaching a search engine reputation campaign, as the utilization of multiple media types and content formats will provide a search-engine-satisfying variety of sources when optimizing for the target search query.

Query Deserves Diversity (QDD)

Search engines attempt to diversify search results when a search query might have more than one meaning, or the user behind the search might have more than one intention.

When someone searches for a term like "java," the intent might be to learn more about Java programming, or the island Java, or the beverage Java. A search engine could just show the most relevant and important results for the most popular meaning (most likely Java programming in this case), but some searchers might be more interested in coffee or the island (Bill Slawski). Diversity in the search results may serve the total audience more efficiently.

A search for "tsunami" might call for scientific studies, recent news, and images of catastrophic wreckage, government warnings, or the Restaurant Tsunami Sushi. Providing only one source of information or type of results would drastically underwhelm the audience with the variety of information sources required to fully answer the search question.

A search for a business or person's name, may suggest interest in a website, social profile, reviews, financial history, matching profile images, news coverage, government records, or videos.

Understanding the nature of diversified search results is crucial when approaching a search reputation strategy. Many people attempt to populate the entire first page of search results with independent websites, or social profiles, resulting in unsuccessful reputation repair because the search engines are determined to deliver a more diversified set of results.

Following chapters describe different options for content creation and distribution that successfully satisfies the diversification needs for a given name search, along with the precise optimization and promotional requirements to achieve authority with those sources of media.

Query Deserves Freshness (QDF)

Search engines pay special attention to search queries that require frequent updating and constantly refresh the list of results based on what is most recent, authoritative, and trending on the topic. Query deserves freshness, is a component of the Google ranking algorithm which assigns weight to a page or document based on its relevance and "recency" – often calculated and scored by how recently a document was created, originally appeared, or has been updated.

Under this concern, documents and website pages with greater "freshness" can achieve a higher placement opportunity than those with less frequent or recent updates. This becomes important depending on the nature of the search query, the user's intent behind the search, and the varieties of information indexed within the relevant context of the searched phrase.

More often than not, search engines favor recent, fresh, and original content regardless of the nature of the search query. Anyone attempting to reshape a search engine reputation (or performing SEO in any search vertical) must consider the freshness factors pertaining to the opposing content in the same vertical.

The likelihood of outperforming a frequently updated or recently published source of content in search is low, unless the content or resource used to challenge the opposing result contains equivalent or greater factors of freshness. Granted, there are many ways to overtake a fresh page of content with old, never-updated content, and the chapters to follow describe exactly how that is achieved. However, going against the grain of ranking factors proves to be too difficult for many inexperienced reputation marketers.

Take for example the case of a negative business profile on Yelp, with frequently updating customer reviews. This is a case of an authoritative site, containing a relevant, optimized page about a business, with strong freshness factors taking place by way of recently published consumer reviews. Every time this page publishes a new user review, the search engines discover more-new-recent information, further satisfying the search engine's decision to serve this page to its users.

Understanding the nature of freshness factors in general, along with how they play a role in the reputation vertical one desires to cleanse and control is vital in the proper engineering of a successful campaign.

Rich Media

Search engines love rich media like videos and images because these media formats provide unique variety to users navigating search results pages for answers. Website pages that contain rich media options for visitors usually gain recognition from search engines in the indexing and ranking process because these pages containing rich media are more likely to serve a user's search query in ways that other pages containing only text content may not.

If all things are created equal between two pages of text, except that one of the pages contains videos, images, and possibly other rich media formats like audio and other downloadable document formats, the page with rich media content almost always outperforms the page without.

Understanding the variety of rich media formats available to users (or likely to be desired by users) within a given search vertical is important for successfully competing for ranking positions against opposing content. Leveraging the power of rich media formats can be done by incorporating them into a webpage or profile. When done correctly, one can experience advantages when these rich media formats are coupled with the plethora of supporting optimizations and inbound promotions necessary to get a particular page to perform in search.

Unique & Original Resources

Search engines assign value to websites and documents that contain of unique and original elements. Throughout the concepts, strategies, and formulas explained in this book, one might detect the unwritten mantra of "Add Value To The Web" – which basically challenges the SEO or reputation agent to create unique and meaningful resources that inherently "deserve" to rank highly in the search engines.

The creation of assets containing unique elements (meaning they possess unique qualities not found on other pages) and are original (meaning they are the exclusive resource for a particular body of text, set of images, or information) is a well-established best practice amongst SEO professionals who understand how to achieve top rankings in search.

Search engines favor unique and original resources because they provide a meaningful contribution to the Internet, and become something "worthy" of serving to users on the search platform. When approaching a reputation management campaign involving content creation strategies designed to infiltrate search results pages, it is wise to ensure that the content, images, videos, links, and other media assets are unique and original.

Personalization

Searches that take place on search engines are usually associated with a browser cookie record or user account search history. When a user performs a search, the search results are not only based on the relevance of each web page to the search term, but also on which websites the user (or someone else using the same computer and Internet browser) visited through previous searches. This provides a more personalized experience that can increase the relevance of the search results for the particular user.

Search engines like Google collect and store historical data around user searches and website visiting behavior to continuously revise and improve the search results for a given query. This process of responding to user behavior to improve results is now deeply integrated into the search engine's machine learning systems, resulting in a constantly evolving data set that contributes weight and relevance to websites being clicked, or visited. With or without account login and authentication, actions taken on the search engine interface are recorded and integrated into the formulas that produce the next set of results. More on the exact contributing factors of visitor behavior will be described in coming chapters.

Understanding SERP's

The mechanical aspects of reputation tactics will be best understood with a fundamental understanding of *search engine results pages* (SERP's), and why certain results appear based on the user's search intent.

User Search Intent

Search query objectives range from research topics, to shopping and commerce, to local business interests, to entertainment or trends. In order to be effective in the creation of content assets for the purpose of penetrating a search environment, one must understand how to create content that answers to the "intention" behind the user's search query. These intentions typically fall into several general categories.

Location Specific Searches

Location specific searches consist of locally driven demand for a business, product, or service that is typically sold or accessed within the nearby area of the user performing the search. Searches that are commonly associated with a location, with or without a search modifier that suggests a specific location, will result in localized results that pertain to the searchers location. Examples of localized searches include dentists, doctors, restaurants, clubs, floral shops, coffee bars, automobile maintenance stations, convenience stores, etc.

Local verticals are often populated with local business results, or information about the product/service/business in that location, or results about the location itself. In these cases, an approach that focuses heavily on optimizing assets with the relevant location factors within the search vertical is most effective.

National Searches

Search queries without the presence of location specific interests will force the search engine to cast a wider net on their indexed resources and produce a set of results void of any location specific criteria. Examples of this include general information on a common topic, research queries relating to trends or news, shopping and commerce products that are typically sold in e-commerce websites, and anything that does not typically require a local resource to correctly answer the searchers question.

National search results can be detected by the lack of location specific nearby results. In general, national search verticals are slightly more difficult due to achieve top rankings in due to the broader set of competing pages for the given search query.

Shopping & Commerce

Any search that suggests commercial or buying intent falls into a categorization of shopping and commerce, particularly keyword search phrases that indicate an interest in physical goods that can be purchased or shipped. Searches indicating this intent are assumed to be best served by shopping related websites such as large e-commerce stores like Amazon, Target, Walmart, or any large or small, publicly or privately owned e-commerce website offering same or similar products to the search query.

Commerce driven searches often produce results from Google or Bing's shopping engine, resulting in the display of specific product images, prices, and links to unique product pages where a visitor can access more information about the particular product they have expressed an interest in. Although there is often a crossover between shopping+local and shopping+informational relevance, searches suggesting interest in purchasable products or services typically result in online shopping options being displayed.

Informational

Research related searches requesting information on a topic, idea, business, person, location, object, or thing, and anything that can be answered by "information" could be categorized as informational. Even if a product search suggests a relevance to shopping and possible intention to purchase goods, the search could also be answered by providing a research paper, product review site, or spec and model information about the product.

How-to, instructional searches on how to accomplish a task or how to do something call for information driven content results that teach or inform the user on the process and steps of the topic being searched. Then again, if Google or Bing have indexed products on the topic (perhaps instructional books or video products) there are likely to be a combination of informational content and shopping options.

Informational search queries typically have the largest variation of results unless the search phrase is so neatly identified that the search engines can precisely answer the search query with one specific type of content. Take for example a search for the word "yoga" - the results include local business yoga studios, informational sites about yoga, medical sites about the health benefits of yoga, purchasable instructional videos on how to do the activity of yoga, and news results about yoga trends.

There are several other possible sub-categorizations of user search intent, such as Entertainment, News, and Trend related, or media type subsets like Image, Video, or document specific requests. The takeaway is that the greater the understanding of the search vertical, the content types, and the intention behind the user's search query, the greater chance one has in influencing the results displaying for that query. Creating content assets that speak directly to the user intentions behind a search is a much easier process than attempting to force-feed irrelevant or subpar content into the keyword space.

How SEO Works

The process of search engine optimization is a vital component to any successful search engine reputation campaign. In order to control an entire first page in Google or Bing with the goal of eliminating something bad, SEO tactics must be applied to existing positive and neutral assets surrounding the negative content that should be suppressed.

Boosting ranking placement for a target property requires precise optimizations to be implemented both on the page property itself and external to the page property. Additionally, well-planned SEO methodologies should be the foundation of all new content and media assets created to infiltrate the search vertical for a given reputation name or search phrase.

Search engines deploy web-crawlers (often referred to as "bots") that scour the world's websites and all their pages. On these websites, the search engine bots read, count, measure, calculate, and score websites as a whole, unique pages individually, using hundreds of ranking factors.

Ranking factors, essentially, are the elements, metrics, and scoring variables search engines use in the algorithms (formulas) that produce the rankings, or sort order, of results displayed for each search. The ranking factors they calculate continue to expand as search sciences adapt to evolving technical elements on websites, resulting in a moving target for anyone attempting to put their finger on a precise weighting and scoring system one can depend on during the SEO process.

In order for search engines to generate a set of accurate, qualitative results for a search word, hundreds of ranking factors are precisely measured, and dozens of robust mathematical comparison calculations have to be processed. In a consideration of relevance for a particular word or search phrase, a website or page is scored individually, and is compared to all its peers (other relevant websites).

Before engaging in what could be considered a surgical approach to reshaping a reputation in search, a comprehensive overview of search engine ranking factors will be helpful in evaluating the suggested actions to follow.

On-Page vs. Off-Page SEO

At this point in the book, several references have been made to optimizations pertaining to the site or page itself, along with the necessary promotions or inbound signals to a given page. These references lead directly to the concepts of on-page (or on-site) SEO, and off-page (or off-site) SEO.

On-page optimizations are things that happen on the site or page itself, whereas off-page optimizations are things that occur externally to the site or page.

Many people approaching the SEO process believe that SEO begins and ends with the site or page only, and fail to consider the dozens of factors the search engines consider as externally referencing signals to a page or site.

An appropriate visual illustration of value pertaining to on-page vs off-page, would be an iceberg. The tip or top of the iceberg above the water represents the on-page factors, and the bottom part of the deceivingly massive floating iceberg represents the ranking factors in the off-page group.

A search engine reputation management strategy that does not incorporate both strong on-page optimizations and aggressive off-page promotional strategies will fall short of producing the desired ranking results for sites or pages targeted for top positions.

The following sections are a technical journey through ranking factors aggregated through years of researching search patents, testing optimization and promotion strategies to prove effective rank manipulation technology, and further validation through the analysis of tens of thousands of search phrases and hundreds of thousands of top ranking page comparisons. In other words, the following ranking factor overview is not theoretical in nature, but rather a scientific process by which theories and facts are acquired, and checked for accuracy.

On-Page SEO Ranking Factors

As mentioned above, onsite factors are elements and features that exist on a site or page itself. These factors are by and large used to score metrics relating to relevance, quality, freshness, trust, age, usability, and the overall usefulness of a resource or document.

While the proceeding factor set does not consist of all on-page variables considered by search engines, the following are the more dominant among the many.

Domain Age

Website age plays a role in the ranking formulas for major search engines as an indicator of website trust and legitimacy. Age is determined by the original domain registration date, registered owner transfer date, or first date of a website's content or pages being included in the search index.

Similar to a business that has been in existence for a long period of history, or as an older man or woman might be assumed to have a higher level of intelligence of wisdom, so do older, more aged websites inherit an assumed higher likelihood of trust. Websites with higher trust signals tend to perform better in search results.

Website Size

The size, or number of pages a website has indexed in the search engines attributes an additional element of weight and authority. The larger a website is, the more domain authority and weight each page potentially has. Depending on how the website is developed, and the linking relationship between pages, a website can funnel authority and relevance between pages in such a way that automatically generates top positions in search.

Large sites like Yelp, Amazon, CNN, New York Times, and Facebook have millions of pages and tremendous domain authority, and are perfect examples of how website size can influence search placement. Of course there are dozens of factors that contribute to top placement, however in general a website's size can be a large contributing factor in the amount of authority and resulting top placement it can achieve with its pages in search. Future sections discuss how to capitalize on the size and weight of these mega-sites for reputation management strategy.

Website Technology

The website development industry is constantly pushing the boundaries of cutting-edge technologies in all aspects of website design and usability, programming and code standards, server solutions and data storage, and so much more. As web development technologies advance, so do the search engines in their ability to score and rank websites based on the newer standards of website technology.

Website technology typically governs the overall usability and visitor experience of a website, and because visitor experience is also a major ranking factor, the technology with which a website is built does not get overlooked. There are many aspects of a website's technology that pertain to search optimization, such as clean well-written code, fast loading pages, mobile friendly aspects that make the site more conveniently accessible on Smartphones and tablets, the efficient management of data, architecture of server solutions (technology stack), and much more.

The best approach to technology optimizations from a search engine ranking perspective is to consider it as a holistic process that requires an all-encompassing calibration of the current best practices and standards in website development. To those not familiar with website design or not driven by any desire to create their own website(s), this is not a constraint in the reputation management process.

The good news for reputation management campaigns is that the creation of new websites, or the technology optimizations of existing websites, is not a requirement for success. Many of the sites and platforms recommended as a component of strategy already have all the necessary technology in place.

Website Content

A website's content is one of the largest, if not most important on-page factors for top rankings in search. Content refers to any text or image material present on the page or website under consideration. Remembering that the search engines are seeking to correctly answer user search questions, the text information available on a website is primarily what constitutes relevance for queries the search engines are attempting to serve.

Within the realm of content evaluations, there are many factors that relate to relevance, quality, uniqueness, originality, and usefulness. Text content was among the first things search engines learned to analyze and score, largely because the Internet has always been about information sharing. Reading and understanding the information contained in text content has always been a high priority for search engine companies. Fast forward to our current day, search engines have the ability to calculate precise intricacies within a body of text or collection of documents.

Content Relevance

Beginning with relevance, the search engine's first order of business is to determine what a page of text content is about. Essentially, what the content says, and what topic or topics it covers. The topical nature of a page gives the algorithm a base set of relevance criteria from which it can begin processing the many other comparison calculations it requires to effectively position that page in search.

The relevance assigned to a particular page for a given topic or search query used to be primarily calculated by looking at word densities and attributing scores for the page based on the prominence, frequency or placement of words within the text, however in our current days of semantically driven search algorithms, the combinations of related words attribute most of the relevance signals for a given page.

Search engines are beginning to focus heavily on rewarding pages that cover topic clusters, rather than a one-word subject. A writer familiar with the full scope of possible related terms for a given topic, such as synonyms, nouns, adjectives, and common semantic relationships typical found in authentic content for the given subject, will have an advantage producing text content the search engines reward with a higher relevance score.

Experts in search optimization refer to this process of semantic search optimization and word groupings as "LSI keyword optimization". LSI stands for "latent semantic indexing" which is a process by which search engines determine the relevance score for a page based on the presence of common industry or technical topic related words being present within the text.

"You shall know a word by the company it keeps"   - John Rupert Firth

Content Quality

The quality of content is an important factor. A page of text that is written poorly with incorrect grammar will rarely achieve a top position in search because it is unlikely to satisfy the user's search query, whereas a page of text that is well written and contains no grammatical errors promises to be a more appropriate document for a reader.

Content Uniqueness

Text content that is identifiably unique across the full index of similar, relevant pages in the search engine will score much better than a page containing matching or duplicate attributes from other pages in the index. The logic behind rewarding uniqueness is based on whether or not the page of text adds anything unique or valuable to the web.

Duplicated content is perceived by search engines as unnecessary clutter in the index of results and is actively demoted in ranking position in an effort to keep all top ranking pages uniquely valuable for a given search phrase. Duplicate content on a website can actually have a negative impact on a domain's performance in search depending on the volume and dominance of duplicate content in comparison to the amount of content with positive scores for uniqueness.

When approaching text content creation for SEO or reputation management it is important to ensure a 90% uniqueness score in relation to other pages already in the index for a given search phrase. Furthermore, the more uniqueness provided in terms of facts or data will allow a page to be perceived as a uniquely identifiable resource on a topic, as opposed to a page that is contextually different from others, but essentially says the same things.

Content Originality

Original content performs better in search than content that is redistributed, duplicated, or is a curated form of the same content. Again, adding value to the web with unique and original content is important. Search engines will ask the question (mathematically of course) "Have we seen this content before?" and "Was this content found here first?" and "Is this the original source of this text information?"

Content created for the objective gaining top placement in search must be original in nature, and should not be the duplication or closely matching offspring of another resource document already discovered and present in the index.

Content Usefulness

Finally, with all the variables of preceding content ranking factors being met, a body of content may be considered useful for a given search query. Ultimately, usefulness scores are going to be influenced by visitor behavior and the experimental display of the page in search results, and recalculated based on the engagement clicks and visitor retention on the page being served to users. Visitor behavior metrics will be discussed in a following section, but it is important to consider how well a body of text serves a user conducting a particular search.

The length, or volume of text within a page or document may be an indication of usefulness for a given search phrase. Longer pages tend to provide more information on a topic, and cover a broader or more in-depth view of a given topic, resulting in search engines assigning more weight to a page containing more words than one with less. Analyzing thousands of top ranking pages across tens of thousands of searches proves that pages with more text typically outperform pages with less text. Pages with little text are often considered "thin pages" and do not perform well in search because of assumed constraints on providing the user the more useful information for their search.

Images are considered a rich media type of content that are also subject to these measurements of relevance, quality, originality, and usefulness. Search engines have image recognition technology that allows them to make astonishingly accurate guesses as to what objects are displayed in images and they use this technology along with comparing pixel placement within graphics to determine the uniqueness and relevance of an image for a given search query. This means that even if an image is downloaded from the Internet, renamed and resized, and re-uploaded to a different website, the search engines have the ability to determine whether or not that image is unique, original, or relevant for a search query.

Duplicated or copied images provide little if any new value to the Internet, so search engines treat these content assets the same as text. A page with 100% unique text and images is going to perform better than a page full of duplicated text and image content.

Use of Rich Media

Mentioned in previous chapters and repeatedly throughout this book, search engines have the ability to understand, index, and serve various types of media formats. Because different media types provide unique answers to user search questions, search engines reward pages that contain original elements or combinations of rich media. Images, videos, downloadable documents or files, and unique media formats that present information in ways simple text cannot, may be considered rich media.

A page containing a simple block of text but no rich media is not going to perform as well as a page containing the same text along with a plethora of images and videos. Content scoring factors apply to rich media, so there is more value associated with higher quality, unique and original, relevant rich media elements within a page.

Creating SEO and reputation management content assets with the inclusion of rich media formats is a smart way to provide something unique and original to a search vertical. Coupled with the other on-page and off-page tactics explained, these types of pages tend to achieve higher rankings much faster.

Static Quality Elements

Within any target page on a website, there are a series of what would be considered "static" elements. These are elements that are fixed, and unchanging, but could potentially be optimized for better visibility and placement in search. Among the SEO industry, there are sets of common static on-page elements that can be optimized for increased relevance. Some of the most common are:

- Meta Data *(Page titles & descriptions)*
- Heading Tags *(Headlines and sub-headlines)*
- Image Alt Text *(Alternative text seen on hover or describing an image)*
- Image File Names *(search-phrase.jpg)*
- Content Tags *(Defining what a section of content is, article, bio, etc)*
- Breadcrumbs *(Text or links showing a visitors navigation path)*
- Contextual Content *(Text information displayed on the page)*
- Contextual Linking *(Links from one page to another, within the text)*
- External Links *(Links pointing out to other resources or documents)*
- Navigation Structure *(Site architecture and relationship between pages)*
- Anchor Text *(Words used in links point to internal or external pages)*
- Rich Media Content *(Images, video, documents, files)*
- URL Taxonomy *(Web page addresses and the structure of words in URLs)*
- Code Elements *(Structure, quality, organization, compliance)*
- Many, many more..

Dozens more static page elements could be listed depending on the type of site or page under consideration. Often, elements that appear to be static or unchanging may actually be "dynamic" in nature, meaning that they are subject to programmatic changes based on the syndication of content, visitor behavior or engagement on the site, or recent updates from the website owner.

Search engines analyze and calculate the relevance and authority of pages by dozens of factors, so it is important to select and optimize as many elements as possible on any page targeted to serve an SEO or reputation management strategy. Websites, pages, or profiles that provide little influence over these areas of optimization can be a constraint in the process of achieving a top placement. In future sections, optimization friendly platforms are provided with instructions for each.

Website Performance Metrics

Websites and web pages are scored on many factors seen and unseen by the naked eye. Search engines analyze and score a website or page based on factors of performance, the most common of which is site speed. Site speed is a metric calculated based on how fast a website or webpage loads in the browser window. Sites and pages with a slow load time do not typically perform as well as pages that load fast, provided that many other ranking factor criteria is met on the fast loading site or page.

Many additional performance factors are measured, but most of them point back to how well the site performs for the user visiting the website. A fast loading site that serves all of its content, images, and resources to visitors efficiently and without bottlenecks and delays tends to be rewarded higher placement that a website that is lacking in performance.

Visitor Behavior (User Metrics)

"We have always relied on user feedback to improve the quality of our results"
- Google.

Let's face it, search engines like Google are not surveying the world of Internet users about each website they include in their index. Or are they? Certainly not through a typical survey, or user feedback process, however they have many ways to collect "feedback" from visitors on a particular website. Although consistently shifting away from their manual review and more towards machine learning systems, they still use manual reviewers to help train their search algorithms.

Google Analytics, the most widely adopted website analytics software collects library-sized volumes of data on any website on which it's installed, and Google can use this data along with data from other sources, to calculate a user's experience of a website. Other sources of data collection are the actual SERP's pages, the Chrome Browser, and plenty of other data sourcing solutions.

Visitor behaviors (aka "User Metrics") have become a major contributing ranking factor in the organic placement of websites in search, and there are a few primary areas of focus attributing the most informational feedback being used by search engines for the scoring and ranking of pages in search.

CTR (Click Through Rate) From SERP's – Remembering that "SERP's" stands for search engine results pages, the click through rate (CTR) of a page in the search results is a factor in ranking position. The CTR is the percentage of people that click the page listing in comparison to other pages in the results, and the rate and percentage of clicks a page receives is a strong indication of its relevance and value to users searching for a particular phrase.

A high CTR from search results pages indicates that a page is in demand and favored by users searching a phrase, whereas a low CTR indicates that result is not attractive or useful. CTR is a component of "user feedback", and serves as a mechanism of surveying the audience, which the search engines (especially Google) use to validate and calibrate the results they display for given search queries. Creating attractive pages with compelling titles that inspire clicks is one way to have an advantage in the set of results for a given query.

Bounce Rate – A website's bounce rate is the percentage of people that visit the website and immediately leave (typically measured by a threshold of 11 seconds). A high bounce rate indicates a web page is not an ideal or qualified candidate for given search, and can lead to a particular page sliding backwards in search position. Building pages that retain visitors and keep them engaged is very important for achieving and sustaining a top position for a given search query.

Time On Site – Similar to bounce rate, the time a user spends on a website is suggestive of how useful and resourceful a website is. If a website retains a visitor long enough to avoid triggering a bounce rate metric, but only keeps the visitor engaged a fraction of the time users typically spend on sites they visit under the same search query, that website might not be awarded as high of a position in search compared to the websites that retain visitors for a longer period of time.

The influence of this metric on search position is entirely dependent on how well the page accomplishes the user's search objective. It may be that the web page efficiently satisfied the user's question and didn't require a lot of time/retention from the user to correctly answer the search query, in which case the web page may appropriately be awarded a higher position.

Alternative rank position influencing visitor behavior metrics may include things like the number of pages visited, the number of clicks within the page, return visitors to a particular page, comments and engagement within a page, or the amount of the page consumed by the length of scrolling.

Additionally, user metrics include things like navigational searches, which are searches initiated by users requesting a particular page on a defined website.

When the search engine (definitely Google in this case) notices a trend of users searching for a particular page, or combinations of brand/website words that indicate a particular page is desired, this is a strong signal that the page requested is of increased importance to users and will be granted more prominence in matching and related search queries.

In conclusion, dozens, sometimes hundreds of on-page ranking factors are involved with the proper sorting and serving of search results. Knowledge of these factors, mastery over the implementation steps, and intimate awareness of which factors will yield the greatest opportunities for the target search term vertical, are of tremendous value during any SEO reputation management campaign.

The tactical approaches explained in coming chapters provide options to exploit necessary platforms and ranking factors for the greatest possible gains in search optimization for reputation management.

Off-Page SEO Ranking Factors

Search engines like Google and Bing have many difficult responsibilities when it comes to organization and serving the world's information and media, one of the most important of which is making calculated decisions on which websites and pages to present at the top of results for users. Search engines are placed in a position of trust and in many ways provide a public service that all slices of society hold under great reliance.

People rely on search engines to serve correct information for their searches, and they must answer search queries correctly otherwise they fall short of their responsibility and run the risk of becoming known as "misinformation engines."

In order for search engines to effectively deliver on their responsibility in the correct organizing and ranking of information resources, they must consider signals of trust and validity external to a resource or document. Without analyzing signals external to a website or page, search engines are left with only data and information that can be gathered from the website itself.

The building of beautiful, information rich websites is a common skill possessed or accessible by anyone who decides they want to develop an Internet property. In many cases, similar companies within the same industry create a website that closely matches another in terms of informational content and appearance. Frequently, two or many websites exist on a particular topic with conflicting information about a subject. This type of situation can be confusing to a person conducting research, and may result in the person being misled or accessing information that is not authentic, or possibly completely false.

How then does a search engine determine which among the millions of sites are the most authentic, authoritative, popular, and worthy of a trusting visitor's attention? The answer lies within the trust and authority signals that reference a website, page, or document from external sources. These signals range from inbound links from other websites, social media presence and activity, brand or business verification, and many other events that indicate a reference or relationship to a website.

Librarians have always determined the authoritativeness and merit of a book or academic paper by considering how many 'other' documents or books reference it. A study or research paper that receives the most "citations" from other related papers and documents is considered to be the most authoritative on a subject, and so it goes with search.

Links and citations from one website to another are like votes. The more link and citation votes a website has from other sites, the more popular or authoritative the website becomes. However all links are not created equal. Links from other relevant sites and trusted sources lend more weight and authority to a site than links or votes from unrelated, or less authoritative sites.

Links, citations, social shares, mentions, and references to other websites are created in millions every day, hour, and minute, and every link or vote created from one source to another on the Internet in some way plays a role in how the search engines sort and rank their pages. But which links matter? Which links are stronger? What gives a link relevance, and which links are completely ignored? Can links damage a website? How are links created? How can one utilize links most effectively for reputation management and SEO? Does a presence on social media influence search position? Do shares and posts about a website factor into the algorithm? What about a website's brand validity and recognition? Does Google analyze a business and challenge whether or not it is a real company? How can one leverage social media and the branding to influence search position?

The following sections answer all these questions and more. Dozens of ranking factors are involved in the analysis and scoring of links and external signals pertaining to a website's position in search. Everything matters, from the type, timing, sequence, velocity, source, quantity, and much more.

Inbound Link Ranking Factors

<u>Notice</u>: Inbound links (also known as "backlinks") and other off-page signals to websites are a large contributing factor to top rankings in search, however without meeting the basic and advanced criteria of on-page ranking factors, off-page signals are much less effective in producing the desired result. In other words, it's best not to make the assumption that a poorly created website or page containing lousy content will perform well in search by only focusing on off-page factors or links.

What is a link, and what is not?

A link is any clickable text (or image) pointing from one website to another. If the reference to a website is not "clickable" (meaning a visitor can mouse click the link and navigate to another website) then it is not considered a "link." References to websites that are not actually clickable can still have value, and may be in the form of a website or business "citation" which are covered in the Brand Recognition section to follow.

Link Types

The types of links pointing to a website can vary from regular hyperlinks using contextual words or phrases, clickable images embedded in a page or the sidebar of a website, citations from directories, shares on social media platforms, references within documents or wiki type pages, editorial links from news related sites or blogs, links within comments posted by users collaborating on articles, and even .gov government domains or .edu educational or university websites.

Just like search engines categorize different types of content and media, they also categorize and score various types of links differently. Primarily, the source of the link determines its type, such as a "News" related link, but there are additional criteria the search engines consider when analyzing the backlink profile of a given domain or individual page.

Links can have a variety of different attributes such as "nofollow", "author", "publisher", and other tagging attributes used by webmasters as instructions for search engines to properly classify them.

Without going into a tutorial on the HTML (hyper text markup language) used by website developers to build websites and links, there are a few general concepts regarding link types that are important for an approach to linking effectively.

Naturally occurring backlink profiles typically have a combination of different types of links (text, images, nofollow, different sources, etc). The presence of varying link types in a website's linking profile suggests an organic (natural) evolution of links, possibly created by a community of followers and affiliated web publishers. Alternatively, a backlink profile consisting of only one type of link (blog comments for example) does not suggest a naturally occurring placement of links, and leans more towards an obviously manipulated backlink profile engineered to "game" the ranking algorithm.

Be cautious creating unnatural backlink profiles with obvious footprints the search engines might view as rank manipulation. These patterns may suggest an effort to game the search engine ranking system and may result in the website being demoted, or at the very least efforts and linking resources being completely wasted inside a strategy that will not be effective. The following sections describe certain footprints to watch out for, and the linking criteria worth considering when conducting a linking strategy.

Although most link authority is strictly attributed to the source of the link, certain link types inherit more trust and validity than others, and some fall under no risk of penalty altogether. In general, contextual hyperlinks from quality content publications on trusted websites, and image links with only the image containing the referring link are quite safe and rather effective, whereas an abundance of wiki-related links, junk article links, or blog comments tend to suggest a spamming approach.

The best approach to establishing link types is to ask the question, "What is the natural, legitimate reason this site/page/source would provide this link?" Granted, there are many ways to mass-produce an abundance of links while avoiding running into trouble with a search engine penalty, and many experts in the field do this with great skill.

In some cases, it is impossible to generate enough "natural" links for all the 10 properties one needs to strengthen on the first page of search results, and the only way to effectively control all the rankings for an entire search vertical is through a robust linking methodology involving many manual and automated linking processes and link types. For the purpose of education and transparency, this book details what those processes entail and the criteria that must be followed in order to be effective.

Link Authority

All links are not created equal. A link from a government website is not the same as a link from as a link from a news website, which is not the same as a link from a random blog. Link authority (essentially a metric of trust, and strength) is derived from a number of factors, and the more authoritative a link source is, the more weight (or "juice" as industry people like to say) the link passes to the linked website or page.

Domain authority (DA) plays an important role in the value of an inbound link, as does page authority (PA), which is the authority of an individual page. The primary factors involved in calculating link authority are based on the popularity, strength, and relevance of the site passing the link citation.

Popularity is determined by the number of links pointing to the site, the number of people or audience size the site maintains, and the amount of traffic the website receives and sustains. The strength of the linking website is calculated based on the quantity and authority of the sites linking to it, and a page on a website has an authority score which is calculated by how many other sites link directly to that page, along with considerations for how many times the site itself links to the page. The relevance of a link is determined by how closely related the linking page is to the linked site in terms of contextual relevance and the topical nature of the site as a whole.

Typically, more relevant, high authority links acquired to a page translates into higher authority and resulting ranking position for the page receiving the links.

Link Relevance

Link relevance is rewarded, and justifiable deserves a higher validation score in the backlink profile of a given website or page. As mentioned previously, academic research papers and books that are neatly focused around specific subjects of study and are consistently referenced by related document citations maintain a higher level of accreditation and validity. Websites and individual pages on websites are scored based on link relevance factors that validate the authenticity of the content or material on the website or page.

Relevance can be calculated based on a number of obvious and not so obvious factors. In general, a website's relevance to a topic is determined by the content that exists on the website, the volume or quantity of pages that contain content focused on the particular topic, and the quantity and topical nature of sites linking to it. A website may be dedicated to a primary industry or type of information, and unique pages on a site may have the same topic or a variety of topical relevance.

An editorial website may cover a wide range of industries, topics and concerns, but may also publish a unique page on a given industry and topic. If this unique page links to an external website or page, it passes the same relevance inherent in the link source page. Links from related "content" is important, and links from related "websites" are even better. So even if the website as a whole is not perfectly matching the desired topic relevance, if the page the link is coming from is focused on a relevant topic of information, it still passes a relevance score. However, a link coming from a website that is a 100% match to topical relevance, may pass a higher relevance score to the linked website or page, based on the overall relevance of the domain sending the link.

The logic behind link relevance is designed to score websites and pages based on how many industry or topic related external resources link to it. This same logic also seeks to discount or demote value from irrelevant or unrelated link sources. Here's an example of how link relevance might be measured:

Imagine a local dentist website receives a link from several medical websites, several links from a blogger's website who focuses all of her content around the medical science of dentistry, and a link from a local floral shop website. The links from medical websites and the medical blogger are hyper relevant to the dentist because of the industry focus and topical nature of the websites and the content they contain, and the link from the local floral shop website does not carry as much or any relevance to a dentist.

However, consider this scenario - the floral business had a hungry customer who decided one of the holiday pumpkins on display would be a tasty snack, and he lost a tooth in his aggressive pursuit to devour a pumpkin. The webmaster behind the floral shop's online blog decided to publish an article about this bizarre event amidst the garden of flowers, and the subject of the article was an announcement offering any dentist in the area a free bouquet of lilies if they would be willing to tend to the poor (and hungry) man's tooth. The dentist nearby commented on the article, posted his website link, and just like that the floral shop website provided a relevant link to the dentist.

All things considered, relevant site links are better and contribute more value in the linking process when the objective is to climb ranking positions for a given search query or topic, but many unique and creative circumstances exist for creating link relevance.

Link Quantity

The number of links pointing to a website or page on a website are an indication of popularity, and the overall quantity of links is an important factor in the process of achieving and sustaining top positions in search. A website or page with more links than another website or page, is presumed to be a more widely cited resource, and therefore more popular/desired/authoritative for a given topic or search phrase. Of course, all other factors of content relevance and link authority apply, but in general, the more links the better.

While it may be tempting to just create more and more links, there are some logical contingencies around link quantity, which govern the validation of link counts for a given website or page. Websites with high visitor traffic, many pages, and a history of inbound links, would naturally acquire a gradual or possibly rapid influx of new links. However a new website, with no visitors, and only a few pages, might not "naturally" acquire very many links to it within a short period of time.

Many so called "SEO Experts" blast new websites with volumes of links that appear unnatural and do not validate against other measurable factors. There are layers of logic involved in the justification of linking strategies that determine whether or not a high or low volume of links should be present in a given search vertical.

A search vertical might have an extremely small audience; comprised of only a few small businesses who are receiving no links whatsoever to their websites. If a new player enters the space and starts generating hundreds or thousands of links to a new website with no correlating traffic or volume of pages to link to, this might not appear natural. Then again, if that same new player distributed a press release to hundreds of news sites and Google could detect the visibility and reach of the cited business in the news, and possibly throughout social media channels, then an influx of new links might be appropriate.

Chapters to follow describe methods to hack link volume thresholds in order to bypass the risks involved with aggressive linking strategies, and for many reputation management campaigns – this is the only way to effectively infiltrate a search phrase vertical with new websites or content.

Referring Domain Links

Link quantity is important, but the number of linking domains is a much stronger signal that the sheer quantity of incoming links. Individual, unique domains are a link metric worthy of extra attention, because each unique domain that links to target website or page carries a unique vote, whereas many links from the same website domain carry many of the "same vote".

Many web developers, SEO people, and reputation managers have the ability to build new websites with thousands of pages overnight. There are many automated ways to accomplish the publishing of thousands of new "pages" on a website very easily.

If it was possible to manipulate search rankings by deploying a website with thousands of pages linking to one target, well.. the SEO industry would be a lot like it was in 2002.

Today, the criteria governing the value of links from one website to another is carefully engineered to disregard many links coming from the same website, and places more weight on the total number of referring domains rather than the total quantity of links that point to a website.

There are some exceptions to this rule when it comes to certain social signals and editorial/news linking opportunities, which the following sections do explore. The best mindset to maintain about link quantity is to count the total number of referring domains providing links, rather than the overall total number of links.

News Links

Links to a website from news sources are a special type of link that carry a unique sign of authority and trust to a website. A news link can be acquired by a website being the focus of a press release or editorial article published by an editor at a news agency or media site with "news" attributes associated with the content. Of course, in order for a link to be considered a news link it must be present and clickable in the content on the news site.

The logic behind weighting news links differently than other editorial content links is based on the general assumption of popularity, trust, validity, or importance of anything featured "in the news". News websites are often highly reviewed, manually edited, rigorously fact checked, and often maintain strong audience retention. News websites often have high domain authority based on how many other sites link to them, and usually have hundreds of thousands, if not millions of pages in the search index.

Not all sites and content appearing to be news related are truly considered "news", so it is important to validate news related articles by confirming a presence in the News search feature of the search engine. Only then is it truly considered news (for linking concerns).

Same Country Links

Links from the same country or language are more relevant than links from another country or different language. The logic behind weighting same or different country links should be obvious. A website for a business based in Canada or the United States of America receiving links from websites based in China or Russia would only make logical sense if the business was involved in some form of international activity or crossing country borders with its products or services. A local business receiving links from a foreign country would make little, if any logical sense.

Some websites have multiple language features and different domains or pages dedicated to serving content to international audiences and in these cases it might make sense for certain pages on a domain to receive links from websites in other countries. Alternatively, a website might be so large, with a presence in multiple countries, that links from any source location are considered valuable and relevant because of historical linking trends relating to the domain and its content.

Similar to other link factors, the criteria for links coming from the same country or different countries are based on clear logic, but also remains flexible based on a variety of conditional factors. As a general rule, same country links are more valuable than links from other countries.

New vs. Aged Links

Newly acquired links indicate current or recent popularity and interest, while aged links also carry weight derived from their essence of permanence. A website or page receiving an influx of new links pointing to it indicates a growing, consistent audience interest, and the continuous appearance of new links is a velocity metric the search engines measure to validate the perpetual importance of a website or page.

Aged links carry unique value in a backlink profile, and every day/month/year they remain in place the more they contribute value to the page or site they link to. There are many logical reasons an aging link will provide more value over time.

The longer a link remains in place, the stronger probability of the linking site's age increasing, therefore growing it its own authority and trust and in turn passing more trust signals to the page or site it links to. The longer a link remains on a page, the higher likelihood of other sites creating inbound links to that page, in turn strengthening the authority and trust of the linking page and passing more authority over time to the page or site being linked.

For those looking for ways to shortcut the aging and authority process of linking pages, strategies are provided in some of the more tactical tiered linking approaches in coming chapters.

Link Velocity

Among the many linking factors crucial for achieving top rankings in search for a given page or website, the overall velocity of appearing (or disappearing) links pointing to a source is an important signal the search engines consider in the real-time sorting and serving of pages.

Link velocity is the speed at which link signals trend in a certain direction. A rapid increase of new links from new sources is a positive (increasing) link velocity, whereas a steady disappearance of links represents a negative (decreasing) link velocity. The steady increase and growth velocity of new links pointing to a source page or website send a strong signal to search engines that the linked page or website is of increasing importance. A disappearance of links, possibly by way of webmasters or bloggers removing links to a source, indicate a signal of decreasing importance or popularity.

Positive link velocity is generally good, negative link velocity is generally bad. In some cases, it is necessary to decrease link velocity to stabilize a backlink profile, and in other cases it is necessary to increase velocity. In recent years, many website owners have been unnecessarily led down a path of link removal services offered by industry pirates threatening website owners about pending Google penalties.

Link removal has its place and importance in some instances, but like many SEO practices the circumstances that warrant link removal have been wildly misinterpreted and the value and necessity of link removals has become severely convoluted. Many people do not realize that link removals and link disavow processes manufacture a negative link velocity, so its no wonder why so many website owners are scratching their heads wondering why they "still do not have their top rankings back" after removing all their "bad links". As mentioned above, link removals and disavow processes have their place but should only be initiated by an experienced hand – a hand that is also capable of counteracting the inevitable negative link velocity resulting from disappearing links.

Very few SEO or reputation management professionals understand link velocity with the level of intimacy or sophistication needed to effectively control or shift trends in link profile evolution. Some experts in the field operate in markets with high stakes, and there are some who can watch for deficiencies in competitor link velocities and exploit these vulnerabilities as opportunities to spike the intensity of inbound links pointing to the pages used for search position competition, and overtake competitor rankings permanently. Probably sounds a lot like war; For some, it is.

Link Sequences

New links appear for a number of reasons, at varying times, from different sources, and take on many different formats. The sequence of appearing links, which includes the source, type, timing, format, and quality of links, is a carefully monitored and evaluated component to link scoring.

The sequence of appearing links to a website or page might vary depending on the nature of content on the page being linked, the recency or freshness of the page being linked, the business or industry climate for the website being linked, or the audience behavior associated with the website target. The sequence of appearing links including the source, type, timing, and format of links, can indicate a natural or unnatural evolution of links.

Search engines (ESPECIALLY Google) have what they refer to as "link spam" prevention algorithms engineered to detect unnatural patterns in link trends to a website, and the sequence of appearing links is often the first algorithmic trigger point where link manipulation can be detected. The built in logic (actually machine learning A.I. systems) designed to detect link spam watches for patterns, and builds models of acceptable link patterns based on what is typical and normal for a site in a given industry, of a particular size, retaining a certain visitor audience, about a particular topic of interest, with a certain age, and possessing a certain link profile history.

Detectable inbound link patterns are the number one killer of otherwise strong SEO strategy for a target property. A sequence of appearing links from the same source over and over, or in a rapid influx from the same source, would need to be validated by layers of logic justifying links from that source over time or all at once. Similarly, links from different sources that say the same thing (see Link Anchor Text), use the same content, or otherwise "appear" the same for the search engine, are also a detectable pattern.

Alternatively, links appearing from a variety of sources, embedded in uniquely different content, appearing differently using different anchor text or a combination of relational tagging, suggest a more natural sequence of inbound links to a source. More on this topic of acceptable patterns will be provided in the Link Footprints section to follow.

In general, inbound link sequences are important to monitor because an unnatural link pattern can deconstruct the entire progress of a ranking strategy for a target page or property.

Also, the sequence of appearing links should appear naturally, at least within the logical guidelines the search engines follow. For example, a linking strategy that begins with the distribution of a press release, followed by signals from social media sites, paired with a combination of blogger links and article posts, and maybe some high authority blog comment links, may appear natural based on the initiation of links via socially driven sources of website visibility. Whereas a linking strategy that comes out swinging with thousands of blog links or only one type of link, or a random spike of the same links in one day (shame on you, lazy linkers) with nothing to justify increased popularity is likely to trigger the algorithm thresholds for link sequence invalidation, and many links will be completely discounted, or worse they might penalize the linked target.

There are ways to properly surge link volumes to a website, ways to carefully calculate whether or not a linked page or website can receive a surge of new links, and ways to manufacture and exploit the logical reasons why a page or website might warrant an influx of new links, but these are all things that require a steady hand, a deep knowledge of linking strategies, a team or tools, and resources to allocate towards links.

Link Authority Truncation

At this point in the book, many variables involved in calculating the value of a link have been provided. Another technique search engines use to score a link is a process of evaluation that determines how many links point to a link. In other words, the amount of second and third layer votes supporting a vote is a determining factor of a vote's strength.

The truncation of link value (or PageRank) is a process by which the search engines may remove the value of direct contribution for the first level of links pointing to a website or page, and score a website or page based on how many reinforcing links point to its incoming links. This is a method developed by engineers in an effort to combat link spam and promote a safer web experience.

The logic that fuels link authority (or PageRank) truncation is based on a concept suggesting that a link is more valuable and trusted if it comes from a source that is determined trustworthy based on how many links it has pointing to it. A good example would be a link from CNN.com versus a link from myhomemadeblog.com – CNN.com has millions of links pointing to it from thousands of different websites around the world, whereas a small blog might only have a dozen or so links pointing to it. Obviously without a link from CNN.com a website would not receive the pass-through value of all the links pointing to CNN.com, but if a website did receive a link from CNN.com, depending on the type of link and where it was placed, it would inherit a fraction of the CNN.com domain authority value derived from all the links pointing to CNN.com.

This method of validating link authority by discounting the first level of links helps avoid a cluttered search results page, by preventing spammy links from controlling top rankings for sites or pages that do not deserve to be there. There are many methods and automated tools that build thousands of first tier links with the click of a button, and while there are ways to use these tools effectively for PageRank passing and increasing ranking positions, most people use them incorrectly and end up doing more harm than good.

When it comes to domain or page authority manipulation by way of link building, consider this concept:

You're only as good as the links pointing to your links.

Link Anchor Text

Anchor text is the clickable text that links from one website to another. The anchor text used in links pointing to a website provides a search engines information about the content or data that can be found at the link destination, or linked page. Search engines like Google and Bing have always considered the anchor text pointing to a website or page for determining relevance and relationships between pages within a website and external to a website. The ranking factor criteria pertaining to anchor text have undergone many evolutions, and continue to be adjusted based on preconfigured standards as well as machine-learned expectations for what is natural or appropriate for a given website or page.

Many people in the SEO industry remember the days when anchor text was a component to the SEO process that was easy to control and manipulate. Many of the same people are haunted by the changes to anchor text ranking factors made in the year 2012 when Google released their "Penguin" algorithm, a formula to combat the manipulation of rankings through link spam.

One of the major focuses of the Penguin algorithm was designed to penalize websites that had an over-optimization of anchor text. An over-optimization of anchor text simply means that the website had too many links pointing to it with anchor text saying the same thing. Since the release of the Penguin algorithm, website owners have been receiving "Unnatural Link Penalties" from Google, which suggest that links appear unnatural due to the sources, anchor text, sequence, or many other criteria Google uses to evaluate and invalidate links pointing a domain.

Link penalties issued from Google can result in a demotion of ranking position for a given page or the entire website as a whole, and have caused many business owners and webmasters horrifying problems with search optimization and business growth strategies. Anchor text, is the number one offender in the link penalty phenomenon, largely because it is the easiest variable for search engines to track and measure in the evaluation of links.

Without going to deep into what was, or how it used to be with linking and anchor text, it is important to understand that the days of blasting a website or web property with the same keyword or search phrase anchor text are over (unless all you care about is Bing). The presence of the target search term in the anchor text pointing to a page or website once served as a means to boost positions for that page or website very easily, but no longer maintains the effectiveness it once did.

Today, naturally appearing backlink profiles consist of a wide range of different anchor text combinations, and smart SEO or reputation management professionals know that in order to be effective with any type of linking, one must use a wide variety of clickable words and phrases in order to avoid creating a pattern that forces the search engine to discount links or penalize the target page being linked to.

The logic governing safe anchor text linking answers to the expectations search engines have for websites possessing backlink profiles that contain a natural occurring combination of words and text links pointing to them. A website that has thousands of links using all the same anchor text does not appear natural, whereas a website that contains a variety of branded words, URL links, generic terms like "click here" and some keywords, does appear more natural.

The presence of certain words in anchor text profiles are important, such as "branded" words suggesting that people are linking to a business, the presence of keyword variations and desired search terms to increase the relevance of the targeted page for a given search phrase, the presence of non-optimized generic words such as "check this out" or "I like this" indicate people are linking naturally, the occurrence of what are considered "naked URL links" which is just the web address of the page as the anchor text suggest that other websites are simply adding a hyperlink to a page and not concerned with the rankings of that page, along with many other word combinations and variations that amount to a natural (appearing) backlink evolution to a target.

Here are some suggestions for sculpting anchor text links that can help with branding, optimization, and variation:

- Naked URLs *(http://domain.com)*
- Brand & Branded Terms *(domain name, brand product)*
- Keywords *(keyword, keyword variation)*
- Keywords with generic variations *(click here for "keyword")*
- Keywords with positive sentiment *(favorite "keyword", best "keyword")*
- Keywords with stop words *(looking for "keyword", find a "keyword")*
- Generic words *(click here, visit website)*
- Generic words with positive sentiment *(OMG! My favorite site)*
- Capitalizations, punctuation, and other formatting *(Keyword!, bold, etc)*

In terms of which variations to use more often than others, and what is appropriate or naturally appearing, the safest approach to anchor text density is to lead with branded terms and naked URLs as the dominating inbound link anchor text pointing to a website or property. Read that again! This is the most important thing to learn about safe linking.

Link Footprints

Search engines monitor patterns in links pointing to a website or page for the purpose of validating or invalidating a link, or group of links. Some patterns in backlinks are good, and some can be very bad. A good pattern might include a consistent appearance of links from relevant sources and content on a particular topic, or a combination of news links and social links all appearing in related sequences. A bad pattern, meaning the pattern will likely result in links being penalized or ignored, might include an appearance of links using all the same anchor text, all the same types of sites, or coming from the same article published on many sites, or all the links are coming from unrelated or spam related websites.

Link footprints (bad patterns in this context) are typically best avoided by ensuring there are no obvious signs of link manipulation taking place. A bad pattern could arise from many obvious and less obvious reasons. Obvious patterns include the repeated use of a specific anchor text, the consistent use of matching text content where links are found, the repeated use of the same 2 or 3 links in articles where the links are found, the same link attribute values for title="keyword" and alt="keyword" found within the link code, the same website or type of website linking over and over, etc.

Automated linking tools are the biggest offenders of generating unnatural link patterns, and are precisely what search engines aim to defeat in their efforts to combat link spam. Automation tools have the ability to generate articles, posts, links, and linking tiers in mass quantities by exploiting open publishing permissions on public or privately owned websites. Most people use these types of tools recklessly and without the necessary experience or finesse required to leverage the power of content syndication tools. Not to say they do not have their place of value in the SEO or reputation management process they most certainly do. Some SEO and ORM campaigns require so many links, and so quickly, the only possible way to effectively deliver a controlling influence over 10 results listings in the search engine is by way of linking automation and content syndication. More will be provided on these options and tactics later in the book.

Link Indexing

Links, similar to websites, pages, images, videos, and other types of Internet media, find their place in the search index. In general, a link only counts for a website if it is included in the search index. The first indicator of a link being included in the search index is if the page it exists on is included in the index. A page can be checked for indexing by searching for the full URL of the page in the search engine. If the page comes up first, or is obviously included and served by the search engine, then links on that page can be considered indexed. If the page is not present in the index, it is safe to assume that links on that page are not indexed or being counted.

With the exception of social signals like tweets on Twitter and Facebook shares, links to a website must be indexed in the search engine to pass value to a linked page. There are many reasons why a page or link might not get indexed quickly or at all. For example, the page the link is on might be considered duplicate content cluttering the index, thin content with not enough information to be worth its place in the index, or the website the page is on has been de-indexed (removed) or has yet to be indexed.

Link indexing services exist for SEO and reputation management professionals generating a massive amount of links, and these services and solutions are more of an underground solution for the mass processing of aggressive linking strategies.

Social Signal Ranking Factors

The growth of social media activity has introduced a whole new phenomenon of digital information sharing, and has provided another opportunity for search engines to improve the quality of search results. Information, website links, images, videos, and references to resources shared on social media sites like Facebook, Twitter, Google+, Pinterest, and other platforms provides search engines a fire hose like volume of data to analyze about websites, industries, audiences, and trends.

With such a high volume of informational transactions taking place on social media platforms, the search engines have had no choice but to respond to these data sources by building them into their search ranking algorithm. In many cases, news and information is shared on social media before its published, or ever published on a regular website or news site. Nowadays, if an earthquake or Tsunami occurs, people Tweet and post to Facebook about it within seconds. Search engines have access to this data and can utilize these real-time updates to polish search results into a more meaningful experience for users performing searches.

A "social signal" to a website is any metric of value that takes place on a social media site that can be tracked, measured, and attributed to a website or source of information. People share/post/tweet/pin things they care about, enjoy, want others to see, or think are important. Search engines are wise to respond to these signals of community driven demand, and they have the ability to score and rank websites and pages based on the sums and recency of social indicators of importance associated with them.

Social Signal Types

There are many types of social signals the search engines monitor for a given website from a particular social media platform. The most popular and commonly used social channels like Facebook, Twitter, Pinterest, and Google+ are the primary channels of social data with which the search engines adjust and score ranking positions for websites and pages in search.

Facebook allows users to post links as updates to their profiles. This "Facebook Share" carries as signal of authority to any link a user includes in this update. Any likes, reshares, or comments committed to this user's post including a website link, are also attributed back to the website being linked. In some cases, one Facebook share including a link can result in hundreds or thousands of Facebook signals being sent to the page or website that was linked. Facebook signals can be generated directly on the Facebook website or may originate from the actual website or page via a "Share on Facebook" icon or link.

Twitter allows users to tweet links to their profile. This "Tweet" including a link to a website sends a signal of authority to the linked page included in the tweet. Any favorites, retweets, or replies committed to this user's original tweet are also attributed back to the website or page linked in the original tweet. Social signals to a website from Twitter may be generated from the Twitter platform or may originate from the website or page via a "Tweet" button or link encouraging users to share the information to their Twitter account.

Google+ allows users to share posts of content or links to their profile, and similar to Facebook, any activity such as a "+1", reshare, or comment on the post becomes attributed back to the page being linked in the post. Google+ signals may originate from Google+, or the website or page itself.

Pinterest allows users to "Pin" images to their profile, and organize them in what are called "Boards". Pins, often originating from a website or page when a user see's an image they like or when a website owner wants to pin an image to Pinterest, an image can be pinned to a Pinterest account via any number of Internet browser plugins supported by the Pinterest platform. When an image is pinned to Pinterest from a source, the posted image (pin) carries a link back to the source of the image (essentially, the webpage it was found on). This attribution link pointing back to the source webpage is a social signal the search engines consider as a sign of importance for the image and page it originated on.

These are the most commonly measured social media platforms and signals monitored by search engines for adjusting website and webpage ranking positions in search. There are many other social platforms that carry signals back to source pages, such as YouTube, Reddit, Digg, and other less influencing channels that are still commonly used by people with online social interests. Certain platforms like Instagram or Vine do not offer much link or web page sharing, so these platforms are less influencing outside of brand validation metrics that may be derived from a business or person having a large, active audience.

Social Signal Weight

Compared to on-page optimizations and inbound link criteria, social signals carry a significant amount of weight in the ranking process for a given website or page. According to correlation analysis between top ranking pages and social metrics, social signals appear to be a strong influencing factor in the search engine ranking algorithm.

The logic behind weighting social signals with strong importance is suggestive of strong adherence to "user feedback" and community driven sentiment around certain brands, products, pages, or content. If enough activity is taking place on social media platforms, and enough data can be collected and carefully measured about other websites, it makes logical sense to rely on these user-generated signals of importance.

In some cases, social signals can be used exclusively for achieving top positions in search for a website or page, given they are steady and consistently strong in velocity. Alternatively, social signals can be considered as a validation metric to justify inbound links to a website. If a web page has lots of links but no social signals, the web page may not perform as well as another page with less inbound links and more social signals.

Social Profile Influence

It has been stated that "all links are not created equal" in relation to inbound links to a website, and so it is with social signals. Social shares, tweets, pins, comments and other announcements carry a different level of influence depending on the person or entity publishing the update and the platform they do it on.

A post to Facebook initiated by an individual with 100 friends is not as authoritative as a post published by an individual with 5000 friends, or a brand with 100,000 fans. Likewise, a Twitter user that tweets a website to 1 million followers will be more influencing and authoritative than a tweet from a user with 100 followers.

Furthermore, social media users are categorized by search engines according to their relevance to a certain topic or industry, and scored by their unique authoritativeness on a given topic or industry. A social media user that is a frequent publisher on all things relating to cats might not present much value to a sporting goods retailer if he or she sends out an encouraging tweet about their website. Alternatively, if a well-known product reviewer with millions of followers in the extreme sports vertical sends out a tweet about a new product the retailer is offering, that could carry a stronger influence on that brand's website in search because of the relevance.

Social Signal Recency

The nature of social media behavior provides strong signals of current trends and popularity in a real-time context for search engines. People on social media most commonly post and share things that are happening now, important now, interesting now, and want their friends or followers to see now. Something posted or tweeted two years back in time might not have any relevance or importance to what is currently trending or important, in fact it may be completely unimportant or obsolete.

Because of the real-time relevance contingencies binding data collected from social media activity, search engines isolate these signals into what may be referred to as a supplementary index where the data is stored for a period of time, then deleted, refreshed, or no longer considered for the real-time influence of ranking positions. Search engines also use a supplementary index for social media data to prevent excessive data storage demand on their servers, which makes sense considering the never ending Tsunami of posts and tweets that would inevitably clutter data archives and become outdated.

Social signals are important for search rankings, but there is debate about how important they are in the long term. According to social signals testing performed by SwellMarketing.com, social signals as a real-time ranking signal have an influence for approximately 2-3 weeks before the initial potency of impact begins to become diluted. That said, search engines have always maintained historical data for websites and social signals are definitely counted over a long period of time.

Whether or not they purge the actual comments and posts content is questionable, but a website that achieves thousands of social signals over a 1-2 year period maintains those metrics and they benefit the website or web page's ranking. How much these long-term signals influence a property's current rankings depends entirely on the recency of signals associated with other competing websites, market trends, and other factors.

Social Signal Velocity

Similar to link building, velocity metrics apply to social media signals and activity. A rapid influx of social signals from Facebook or Twitter is a strong indicator of current or new popularity associated with a website or web page.

A steady or sudden decrease in social signals to a website or property indicates a decline in importance.

Social signal thresholds are something worth considering as well. One or two posts or tweets are hardly enough of a signal for the search engines to respond to, but 20 or 50 new shares or tweets might be a strong indicator of importance. The more social signals pointing to a website or page the better, and more than a few are needed to effectively influence ranking positions for a property.

Brand Visibility Ranking Factors

Search engines love brands. They provide ways to verify the legitimacy of businesses, and provide steps to follow to prove that websites are associated with a real company. According to recent studies by SearchMetrics and Swell Marketing Inc, search engines reward verified brands and businesses with higher rankings for their websites than websites with no brand visibility or verification. This "brand factor" correlation between top rankings and verified brands has been thoroughly validated through the analysis of websites with top ranking pages across 10's of thousands of search queries.

What proves a website is a brand? Search engines do not have the time or resources to check with the local government to verify whether or not a website or business is a real company, so like most things they calculate, they use algorithmic processes of validation to determine a brand's validity.

Verified Businesses

The first and most obvious method search engines use to validate a business or brand is through their own verification process. Any business can create a business or maps profile on Google or Bing, with the option to provide an official address and phone number. Once the business provides this contact information, a post card can be sent or phone call initiated, with a verification code that the business owner can return to Google or Bing to "verify" its legitimacy.

This is the first and fastest method to verify a business with the search engine, but may not amount to influencing brand factor desired for search ranking priority.

Business Listing Directories

Many business listing sites exist as directories of businesses in specific local regions or for specific industries. Acquiring placement on these directory sites gives businesses (and websites) more citations of their address and contact information, and many provide a link back to the website itself.

There are many services available for creating these business profile pages, and the more business listing references providing the verified business address and contact information, the easier it is for search engines to further validate a business' legitimacy.

Businesses and website owners with reputation management concerns should be cautioned as many of these seemingly harmless directories offer consumer review features and may present more liabilities in the reputation repair or control process.

Business or Brand Citations

Similar to links pointing to a website, a business or brand can achieve more authority in search through business citations on other websites that include the business or website name, address, and phone number (NAP). Business directory sites are a good source of business citations, because they almost always include the business' name, full address, and phone number.

Business citations can also be created by including the NAP in press releases, editorial content, and social media pages. Any profile or property officially representing a business or brand should probably include the full NAP business citation to lend further credibility to the brand or business' legitimacy.

Always include a link to the website where possible.

Social Presence

Most forward thinking businesses and website owners today create a presence on relevant social media channels, such as a business fan page on Facebook, a Twitter account, or Google+ for Business page. Creating and maintaining a presence on social media suggests to the search engines that the business or website is an active player in the industry or subject of focus, and lends credibility to the business or website as being legitimate.

A website or business with a social media presence should properly associate the website with the social media channels by creating a link from the website to the social media profiles, and from the social media profiles back to the website. This helps the search engines confirm the relationship between a website and the social media page.

Content Publishing

Content publishing is not only a function of bloggers and editors at news sites. Businesses can gain brand recognition and authority through the consistent publishing of content on their website and social media channels. If a business in a specific industry is constantly publishing high quality, useful content for an audience interested in relevant topics, it will be recognized as an authoritative influencer in the market.

Publishing high quality content consistently is a brand strategy that can have a strong influence on an SEO or reputation management campaign with the objective to control as much search landscape as possible.

Google publicly states that the more content a business or brand publishes to Google+, the more it (the brand) will become visible in search.

Business Reviews

Positive consumer reviews on business profile sites like Yelp or Google+ can send strong signals of authority towards the associated website. Search engines respond to community driven feedback about websites and brands, and published reviews for verified businesses are factored into search placement, especially for local businesses and maps ranking positions.

Alternatively, low star ratings for a brand and negative reviews with unfavorable sentiment can be interpreted as signals of distrust and suggest a brand is not preferred by its community audience, in which case the business should conduct a positive reviews strategy to counter act the negative impact of bad reviews, or conduct a reputation management campaign and SEO strategy to suppress the negative review content while strengthening the organic rankings of the main website.

Navigational Searches

Searches that suggest a specific brand or website is in demand send signals of authority to the search engines, which they factor into the ranking algorithm and compare to other websites and brands in the same industry.

A navigational search is any search query that indicates a user is searching for a specific brand website or page on a particular website. Navigational searches have emerged as an important ranking factor variable contributing to brand authority in search. There are many grassroots methods for facilitating an increase in business navigational searches, such as conducting marketing messaging online or offline that leads to users searching for the brand in the search engine, as well as guerilla tactics that artificially manufacture brand searches. Artificial methods of brand search manipulation are reserved for the most elite in the industry, and can be directed at many online properties (brand affiliated or not) for the gaming of search ranking positions.

A Surgical Approach

It is time to take action. The following is a battle-tested approach to cleansing and controlling search results for any name, brand, or entity search phrase.

We have explored our digital world, statistics of Internet user behavior, validated the importance of positive reputation, have taken a journey through ethical perspectives on the industry, highlighted search reputation scenarios and problems, typical problem or opportunity websites, explained how search engines and SEO works, took a deep dive into technical ranking factors, and have explained several reputation concepts and strategies.

The proceeding sections can serve as a guide through the anatomy of a search engine suppression campaign, including steps for defining goals, setting objectives, creating assets, strengthening asset authority, and securing a digital search firewall to inoculate against existing and future negative results.

To be clear, the steps to follow are a combination of methods that have been repeatedly proven to successfully suppress and eliminate negative properties appearing on the first or second page of Google, Bing, or Yahoo.

Defining Verticals

The first step in a suppression campaign is to precisely define the search vertical in which one will conduct a reputation repair or control strategy. A "search vertical" is defined as the set of results appearing for any precise search phrase or a specific search engine. The search phrase might be a person's name, a brand, or organization, on the Google, Bing, or Yahoo search engines.

Refer to the steps outlined in the section "Assessing Reputation Damage" and begin creating a log of search phrases that either have a negative listing that needs to be suppressed, and/or search phrases that need optimization and control.

Examples of search verticals defined in the log might be:

- John Doe
- John Doe Company Name
- Company Name
- Company Name Reviews

Note: For each search vertical (search phrase) selected for the campaign, a unique strategy and set of tasks will follow. In the example set of search verticals above, a different suppression campaign would possibly be required for each depending on how well one can optimize assets for all variations of searches.

John Doe (a person's name) calls for a precise strategy that focuses on optimizing for an individual person, which is different than a strategy that focuses on optimizing for John Doe + Company Name, or the Company Name exclusively.

Content assets will have to be created in such a way that speak directly to the user's search query for the person, the person and the brand, just the brand, or the brand's reviews. Opportunities for content asset creation differ for individuals and brands, and review site results are in a category of their own.

Person vs. Brand

Defining a search vertical as a "person" or "brand" search is important because different strategies and opportunities are available for each. Search engines respond differently to different search queries based on what best serves the user conducting the search, and the assets created for the reputation campaign need to be selected according to what search engines prefer to serve for people, versus what they prefer to serve for brands.

In some cases, content assets can be optimized for both objectives and the steps and opportunities for these types of hybrid optimizations will be provided. At this stage, note next to each vertical defined in the set whether it's a person or brand, or both.

Determine User Search Intent

Understanding the "intentions" and needs of the user initiating the search queries that are the target of the reputation campaign is important for a few reasons. Thoroughly understanding the mindset of the people searching with each search phrase will provide an advantage in carefully selecting the right properties to create or promote, the content and information used when building those assets, and will present opportunities to better serve those people (and therefore search engines) with appropriate informational content.

The easiest way to determine a user's search intent is to analyze the current results that appear for the target search phrase. Refer the section "Understanding SERP's" for a walk-through of search engine results pages, and the general different types of results that appear, and why.

Next to each search vertical in the target list, note the type of search results that appear. These might be local, national, business related, consumer related, informational, entertainment & trends, shopping, or reviews.

Industry Topics

Defining the topical relevance for the target search verticals is an important step in being able to effectively create content assets that are properly optimized and relevant for the target phrases.

For each search vertical defined in the target set, list the related industry topics associated with the person, brand, or product of focus. Examples of industry topics could be sports (or more precisely defined "sports/swimming"), medical (or medicine/pharmaceuticals), finance (investing/tax planning), etc.

Having a list of a 5-10 relevant topics for each search vertical will provide convenience during the process of content creation and optimization.

Taking Inventory

Using the search phrase verticals defined in the previous step, begin the process of taking an inventory of search results for each search query. This is accomplished by opening the search engine in the Internet browser of choice, entering the search phrase in the search bar, and making a list of all the organic listings that display on the results page for the search phrase. Organic results are the listings typically below and to the left of advertisements, and for any given search phrase there should be 10 or more results available.

For each of the 10 results in the inventory list for each search phrase, it is important to categorize each as positive, neutral, or negative. The following can serve as a guide in the categorization process that defines the value and sentiment of each listing.

Positive Assets

A positive asset is anything that is beneficial to the person or brand, or positively serves the focus of the search query. Positive assets might include content written in an enthusiastic or positive perspective, images that convey a professional or clean appearance of a person or brand, videos that convey positive messaging to the audience, or anything that speaks highly of the person or brand or represents the subject of the search phrase in a favorable light. Positive assets are sometimes not accessible or owned by the reputation campaign owner, or may be properties that are not currently "positive" but could be optimized for a better representation of the campaign subject.

Positive assets in the list will be a priority for optimization and promotion in the reputation campaign, so label each item in the inventory list that can be considered a positive asset.

Neutral Assets

A neutral asset is anything that is neither overwhelmingly positive nor negative, and does not possess anything substantially damaging or detrimental to the subject of the reputation campaign. Examples of neutral assets might be general articles or listings about a business or person that are not conveying negative sentiment, but do not necessarily praise them either.

Acceptable images, videos, or any web page listings that fit into these criteria could be considered neutral assets. These properties may or may not be owned or created by the subject of the reputation campaign, and may or may not be accessible for on-page optimizations.

Neutral assets often provide exceptional convenience to a reputation repair campaign as they can serve as supplementary resources for controlling the search vertical. Label any neutral assets in the inventory list.

Negative Listings

Negative listings are properties, pages, images, videos, or any digital media that causes damage or presents liability to the subject of the reputation campaign. Negative listings might include news articles, scam reports, review sites, videos encapsulating a customer's opinion, or any of the situations explained in the "Search Scenarios & Problems" section.

Label each negative listing in the inventory list. These items will be considered unavailable for promotion or use in the reputation management campaign, and should be avoided in all efforts throughout the campaign. Remember that repeatedly clicking and accessing these pages sends a CTR signal to the search engines that they are desirable and worthy of their position in search, so be sure to avoid continuous access of any properties labeled as negative listings.

Negative listings will be the focus items for the suppression process, and all efforts in the campaign will be engineered to eliminate these results from the organic listings on the first and/or second page for the search phrase.

Listing Types

The types of listings and assets present in the search vertical are important in the campaign strategy process, because understanding what types of sites exist and which do not exist will provide opportunities for creating similar types of sites that effectively respond to the demands of the search intent, as well as defining any missing asset types that could be exploited to serve the search requests more efficiently.

Listings may be a type of News, Editorial, Video, Social, Professional Profile, Reviews, Blog, or other type of property. The presence or consistency of a certain type of property in a search vertical may indicate that this certain type of property is the best suited for this search query. Alternatively, there may be a combination of different types present, but missing other types like News, Editorial with Rich Media, Social profiles, etc.

There are almost always opportunities to insert a different type of website into the search vertical due to the concept of Universal Search, which is a method used by search engines to display of variety of types of media and content for a given search query. Leveraging the concept of Universal Search will be a focus throughout this approach, so be sure to revisit that section of the book.

Refer to the section "Typical Problem (or Opportunity) Sites" and label each listing with a property type. Make any additional notes appropriate for highlighting consistencies or missing types in the results for each vertical.

Asset Authority

The authority of the websites and pages defined as negative listings will be an indicator of how difficult a suppression campaign will be, and a comparable domain and page authority in positive or neutral assets will be necessary to overtake the negative listings.

In the coming section "Building Asset Authority" there will be many methods described for increasing the authority of assets in the campaign, but in order to understand how much authority and competition one has throughout that promotional process, it can be helpful to analyze the authority of negative listings and the assets defined for promotion.

Several industry standards exist for measuring the domain and page authority of a property, and tools like Majestic.com and the Moz.com Open Site Explorer are common resources that can be used to evaluate the website and web page strength of any item in the inventory list.

DA (domain authority) and PA (page authority) are typical metrics provided by the Open Site Explorer tool, which indicate a website or page's authority derived from external sources of influence like links and social signals. Trust Flow is a common metric provided by Majestic.com, which is a similar function of inbound citation authority derived from external sources.

Asset authority can be determined quickly by using the tools mentioned, along with additional evaluations of domain type, content type, and the source of information. For example, a quick indicator of authority would be the type of website that contains the negative content. A news article on the New York Times, a business profile on a review site like Yelp or the Better Business Bureau, or a publication on a Government website, can all be automatically considered authoritative. Comparing the positive and neutral asset authority to the negative listing's authority is an appropriate step in knowing how much muscle is needed to overtake the negative listing's position in search with a new asset.

Taking inventory of each listing's authority is a helpful step, so be as thorough and detailed as desired because doing so will serve as a guide throughout the process of strengthening asset authority.

Asset Accessibility

Any content that is not owned or accessible by the reputation subject or campaign manager should be labeled as such, and can only be the focus of promotional, asset authority building efforts. Any property or content that is not under the direct control of the campaign managers should be evaluated for potential risks or change, as adjustments by the owner may result in unfavorable outcomes for the subject of the reputation campaign.

In some cases, content that cannot be controlled represents a liability for the reputation management campaign in the event of a change by the owner. Alternatively, any properties or assets that can be accessed present great opportunities for influencing the value they have in the reputation repair process. In some cases, a property may be identified as a neutral asset in the campaign, but could easily become a positive asset with a few adjustments.

Label any properties that can or cannot be accessed or changed. For the ones that can be accessed, identify any obvious fixes or adjustments that should be made at first glance, and refresh these notes after reviewing the "Optimizing Existing Assets" and "Asset Type Optimizations" sections to follow.

Choosing Battles

Any opportunity in life or business should be evaluated for the probability of success, the pros and cons of engagement, and the cost opportunity involved in seeking the desired result or outcome.

In online reputation management, and especially suppression campaigns, it is important to validate each search vertical defined as being worthy of the time, energy, and resources involved in developing and implementing a campaign that will work. It is also important to evaluate how important each search vertical is to the person or business, within the full scope of other opportunities or search verticals, along with an honest appraisal of how probable a successful outcome will be.

Search Volume

Determining the total search volume for a given search phrase defined in the target set is an important step in evaluating how important the vertical is in the scope of reputation opportunities. The "search volume" of a phrase is the number of people searching for the word or phrase in a given month or period, and many tools like the Google Keyword Planner or SEMRush.com are available to conduct this research.

High search volume verticals typically represent a higher priority that lower search volume verticals, because more people are viewing that set of results. However in some cases, a certain combination of words in a search phrases suggests a user intent that is far more important than a possibly less-focused search phrase.

An example of how a vertical with a smaller search volume might trump a vertical with a higher search volume could be the case of "Company Name + Reviews". Typically a company name gets more searches than the company name + reviews, however the people searching for the company name +

reviews might represent an audience that is on the cusp of making a buying decision, or farther down the consumer sales funnel, indicating that these people are seeking additional information they need to make their final decision to initiate a business transaction.

List search volumes next to each defined vertical in the list, and make any notes appropriate for selecting priority.

Content Evaluations

After taking inventory of the positive, neutral, and negative results for each search vertical defined in the list, evaluate the content on each of the inventory items. In the evaluation process, it is important to analyze the quality, length, strength, and sentiment of each property, for all positive, neutral and negative results.

Refer to the section "On-Page SEO Ranking Factors" and evaluate the content on each of the properties in your inventory list for qualities such as the length, the accuracy and usefulness, the semantic relationships of words within the text, the presence of rich media images or videos, and make notes about the nature of the content displaying for each search vertical in the campaign.

Evaluating the qualities and deficiencies of the competing content in each vertical targeted for the campaign is important for understanding how to create or optimize new content that will be able to earn its rightful place in the search vertical. Without understanding the nature of competing content one will have a difficult time creating new content that effectively challenges search position authority, and can lead to many headaches and set backs in the campaign.

In the inventory process, there was a step encouraging an assessment of "sentiment" contained within each property of content in the search verticals for the campaign. Indicating whether the sentiment on a page is positive, neutral, negative, or very bad is helpful in determining how important or useful a page or property can be in the repair process, and whether or not it is a high priority for suppression.

Positive and neutral properties can be used as leverage in the suppression process, as long as the owner of the campaign can be content with the neutral content remaining intact. Some people and businesses desire to develop and promote only the highest quality positive content in a search vertical, and while this is understandable, a campaign that does not leverage neutral assets will likely take longer to completely achieve control.

In terms of suppression priority, negative and very bad sentiment will usually take a higher priority than positive or neutral content, however even within these groupings some decisions may be made about the level of importance each has in the campaign. Considering that every item listed in the inventory has the potential to either be used or not used to gain control over the search vertical, the more items selected for use results in a faster path to control, whereas the more items not used provides less properties to leverage and more properties to create in the process of optimizing the entire first or second page of search.

To illustrate how this selection process might play out in a search vertical with 10 results on the first page, consider a campaign that selects only 4 out of 10 results on the first page as being usable for promotion. This leaves 6 open results that either cannot be optimized or promoted or used as leverage, meaning that another 6 properties must be optimized or created to effectively infiltrate those 6 positions.

Alternatively, a campaign that uses 8 out of 10 results on the first page only requires 2 new properties to be inserted into the vertical to suppress the 2. The 8 out of 10 approach might consist of using both positive and neutral properties for the purpose of control, whereas the 4 out of 10 approach might only allow for the use of the positive assets only.

Defining Goals

The overall campaign should have clear goals and the campaign manager should have subsets of goals to ensure progressive movement towards the overall campaign goals.

Campaign goals might be a simple as having a "Clean Page 1 of Google" or the objective of "Move The New York Time Article To Page 3".

Assuming the campaign manager has already defined the search vertical objectives for the campaign, and organized an asset inventory based on the results for each search phrase, several additional milestones and campaign objectives should be established and tracked to proceed towards success.

Asset Creation

Very few search vertical objectives in reputation management contain all the possible or necessary positive assets required to control the entire page 1 or 2 of search results.

Based on the number of negative listings desired for suppression, and the number of positive or neutral assets available for campaign promotion, a certain number of new assets should be created. Sometimes, there are plenty of positive or neutral assets available on page 1 or 2 of the search vertical to effectively promote them into higher positions and control the search space. More commonly, a campaign is best suited for the creation of new asset properties which the reputation owner can control and own going forward.

From the "Creating New Assets" and "Asset Type Optimizations" sections, define 5-10 property types that will be created for the subject of the reputation management campaign. These assets might include properties that already exist that are underdeveloped and do not appear in the top results (such as a social profile of a business or person), and simply require optimizations and promotion to achieve top rankings, or may include properties that have never been created for a person or business (such as a blog, social profile, or resume site for a person).

Define how many assets will be created, by whom, and by when. Ensure the person responsible for creating the assets follows the guidelines in the "Creating Asset Content", "Creating Asset Images", and "Asset Type Optimizations" sections.

Note: The person responsible for creating text content should be well versed on the subject of the reputation campaign, the industry or topics of focus, and should write with an experienced and professional ability. The person responsible for creating asset images might be a graphic designer, or the subject of the reputation campaign (person or business) might be able to provide original image content. The person responsible for creating and publishing the web properties should have experience with online profile creation, social media, branding and/or marketing so as to avoid any further asset liabilities in the creation process.

Asset Promotion

Existing positive and neutral assets, along with any newly created assets, will need to be promoted to achieve increased asset authority through a process of content marketing, link building, social sharing, and possibly press release strategies. Many resources are described and mentioned as available throughout the "Sourcing Links" section, so it will be important to dedicate a person or group to this process to ensure the successful promotion of assets.

The entire success of the campaign is dependent on how carefully and effectively asset properties are promoted throughout the campaign, so be sure to dedicate a reliable person or group and require them to use the resources and guidelines described in "Building Asset Authority" section.

Decide who will conduct the promotional aspects of the campaign and allocate appropriate resources for them to engage in the processes described.

Campaign Results

Campaign progress should be tracked and accounted for throughout the reputation repair process. The most common and obvious way to track progress is by analyzing the search results page for each of the search verticals identified for the campaign.

Decide who will be responsible for tracking campaign progress and when and how they will report this progress and to whom. Sometimes a screen shot of the search results page is all that is required by the person engaging in reputation management services, or if the person or company is both the owner and manager of the campaign a simple review of the search results page may be all that is required.

Optimizing Existing Assets

In most cases, existing reputation management assets can be optimized for better performance in search. The ability to optimize existing assets is dependent on the accessibility of each property in the list, and the opportunities inherent in each asset property are dependent on the content type and the optimizations that the particular property supports.

Asset Accessibility Options

The accessibility of assets determines whether or not the campaign manager or reputation owner has the ability to improve on a property selected for the reputation campaign. In the inventory process, assets were labeled according to whether or not the campaign manager or reputation owner had the ability to access a property.

The properties that that cannot be accessed should be considered primarily for promotional efforts, and should remain in the target list of assets if they meet criteria necessary for being ranked highly for the given search query.

Properties that are accessible should be improved and optimized according to the guidelines set forth in the "Asset Type Optimizations" for each particular type of property. Social profiles should be optimized according to Social Platform optimization recommendations, and press releases should follow the News type recommendations, etc.

Asset Opportunities

In the world of search optimization, all assets are not created equal. Some properties present greater opportunities for optimization than others, and some assets are contained on sites with greater domain or page authority than others. Identify which assets and properties present the greatest control for optimization influence as well as the size, authority, and likelihood of high rankings for the target property.

In general, assets that are exclusively controlled by the reputation owner or campaign manager present greater opportunities than those that are not. Additionally, assets that support a wider range of on-page optimization opportunities and possess higher domain and page authority represent greater opportunities for the success of the campaign.

To define the greatest asset opportunities for the campaign, refer to the "Asset Type Optimizations" sections to determine which properties support the most on-page optimizations, as well as an analysis of domain/page authority and the property's accessibility.

Asset Liability

A circumstantial paradox exists with certain properties that appear as assets but can actually present liabilities in the campaign. Any property that is not exclusively controlled or influenced by the campaign manager or reputation owner may evolve into a liability for any number of reasons, so be sure the assets targeted for optimization and promotion are either sustainable in terms of quality and sentiment, or exclusively controlled and influenced by the manager or reputation owner.

Asset liabilities can also be presented when optimizations are applied to a property incorrectly, so be sure to follow the guidelines in the "Creating New Assets" and "Asset Type Optimizations" sections to avoid the potential problems with incorrect asset optimizations.

Creating New Assets

The following guidelines and recommendations apply to on-page optimizations for existing or newly created assets, and seek to parallel search engine ranking factors described in previous chapters. Ultimately, the campaign manager or reputation owner should familiarize themselves with the ranking factors explained in previous chapters, as the knowledge of search optimization best practices provides many advantages throughout the process of SEO and reputation management.

General Guidelines & Mindset

The focus of asset creation and optimization should be geared towards providing something uniquely valuable and original in the target search vertical.

Create original, compelling content and incorporate rich media in as many places as possible when optimizing assets. The more content, information, images, videos, and details that can be applied to a property the better. Take advantage of every opportunity available to include more details, information, text, images, and videos. Remember that the search engines are mathematically organized in such a way to reward the most "resourceful" pages they can discover on an existing topic or search. More content and rich media is always better than less.

Control as many optimization opportunities as are available. Refer to the section title "On-Page SEO Ranking Factors" and aim to control as many of the "Static Quality Elements" as possible, especially the title and description of the page, the URL of the page, the headline or sub-headlines of the content on the page, along with any content that can be optimized such as text, images, videos, and rich media on the page. Thoroughly optimize every field within the page or property so that the search engines have no constraints on analyzing the information provided, and so the page scores better than other pages within the search vertical in terms of the amount of information provided.

URLs of pages are often a great opportunity to increase the optimization for a new or existing asset. Many business owners and individuals do not take advantage or URL customization during the initial setup process of a property or profile, and these can often be improved to more closely match the search phrase targeted for the campaign.

Keyword densities within the page are an important aspect of the SEO process. Too many occurrences of the campaign target phrase will cause the page to become over-optimized and will trigger a reverse affect resulting in the page being stuck on page 2 or 3 of the search engine, or may slide even farther down in the search results when inbound links and matching phrase anchor text is sent to the page (Google Penguin Link Spam algorithm).

Control keyword densities on the page by ensuring the most important areas of optimization contain the search phrase and avoid redundancies and unnecessary duplications. Every search vertical is different, but a good safety threshold (and sweet spot!) is 1% to 1.5% keyword density of a search phrase on a target property selected for the campaign. Depending on the total word count of the page, instances of the keyword search phrase may need to be added or removed. Use any online keyword density checker that analyzes visible text and image alt text, or the SEOQuake browser plugin.

Cross linking between properties is a way to cross-pollinate relevance and authority between assets, so use any and all opportunities to daisy chain links to and from assets to each other. This often translates to embedding hyperlinks into description areas of profiles, adding links to areas that typically only ask for the input of text content, or any available link fields provided by the platform.

The exception to this cross-linking recommendation is if the campaign manager decides to create independent websites on registered domains as a method of asset creation. An example of this might be "mydomain.com", "mycompanydomain.com", and "mycompanyreviews.com". If all three of these sites in this example are developed for the purpose of ranking for the same search term, they can be linked to and from other properties (like social channels and press releases) but be sure to avoid linking between them, make sure they all have completely different content, host them on different servers with different IP addresses, and make sure the domains are set to "private" with the domain registrar.

Missing any one of those guidelines is a sure way to kill the potential of many or all of those domain properties in the SEO process. There are unique exceptions to this safety precaution and ways to use domains without following these contingencies but most people make these mistakes in ways that are unrecoverable. Logic: Google only likes to serve one website from the same owner for a given search query, in an effort to diversify results.

Finally, adhere to as many of the described SEO ranking factors as possible and maintain control of the campaign assets in the event further optimizations and adjustments are required. Rarely ever is there an asset that would not benefit from additional optimizations later in the campaign. Refer to the "Campaign Monitoring" and "On-Page Changes" sections later in the book for these opportunities.

Creating Asset Content

Text content published to asset properties is an asset in itself, the quality of which is a strong influencing factor in how well the property performs in search. The quality, originality, uniqueness, usefulness, length, and relevance of text content are very important areas of focus when developing text for asset properties.

Almost all asset optimization methods provide opportunities for inputting text content, in the form of bios, descriptions, articles, or otherwise. Define what asset properties support content and identify the amount of text (word count

/ length) that each property supports and itemize the content pieces that need to be created.

Engage or assign a writer responsible for producing the text content for the campaign, ensure that the writer responsible follows the criteria outlined in the "On-Page SEO Factors" and "Website Content" sections. Support this writer and writing process with details about the reputation subject, industry, or topics, so that the writer can produce relevance content on the subject. Have them make a list of relevant terms associated with the reputation subject (20-30) and have them incorporate these words within the text for each profile.

Ensure that each property receives 100% original text copy that does not match another property or profile. Use copyscape.com to ensure that text content is not a duplication of some other source already indexed in the search engine.

Create asset content promptly and publish it to the properties as quickly as possible. Ensure that keyword densities of the properties are within the 1-1.5% guidelines after publishing the new text to the page, and make any adjustments necessary to increase or reduce the total occurrences of the primary search phrase.

Creating Asset Images/Videos

Most web properties today support images and videos, and incorporating these rich media types is a great way to strengthen the optimization scores of target properties in the campaign. Images or graphics can be sourced or created using a variety of different methods, and like text content, it is important that images meet certain criteria for them to be helpful in the optimization process.

Images should be relevant to the reputation subject, and represent the owner of the campaign in a positive light. Images should also be original and unique, meaning they have never been published to the Internet and have not been discovered by search engines. When possible, images should be high quality and high resolution so they are viewed as quality media by the search engines.

Images and photos can be sourced from the campaign owner, or the reputation manager may manufacture them with a camera or graphic design software. For campaigns focused on an individual or person's name, the best images to use are of the person themselves. With image recognition technology today, search engines can perform facial recognition to determine if the image is really the person. For companies, people-pictures help but are not required. In both cases, additional graphics may be created to support the enriching of content through image media formats.

Existing images can be formatted in special ways to bypass the image recognition technology used by search engines, such as reformatting an image by size, pixel resolution, contrast, horizontal flipping or rotation, and of course renaming the image file and hosting it on another server. To confirm an image has passed the image recognition technology in Google, upload the image to a server, acquire the full source path of the image by right clicking on it and selecting "copy image URL", and then search for the URL in the search box on Google. At this step there may be a "search by image" option provided, click that, and if Google identifies where the image was originally found – the image did not pass the test. If the image does not match a source, consider this image file an acceptably unique image asset for property optimization.

Videos assets can serve as a unique contribution to target properties in an SEO or reputation management strategy. Video producers or contracted media agencies may create promotional or marketing videos. Alternative methods for acquiring video assets might be clients or friends who are willing to give a testimonial or review in the form of video, or any number of online free or paid video production tools like Flixpress.com, GoAnimate.com, Animoto.com, or Fiverr.com

Image and video file names should be optimized with the target search phrase by incorporating the words into the file name separated by hyphens. This file name optimization is an important step in the process of optimizing images for search visibility and relevance.

- search-phrase-name.jpg
- company-name.jpg
- persons-full-name.png
- my-brand-product.gif

The type and quality of image and video content is ultimately under the discretion of the reputation owner and may need to follow certain standards depending on the nature of the business or professional stature of the person for whom the reputation campaign is for.

Asset Type Optimizations

By now it has become clear that many different types of web properties exist, and many forms of optimizations are necessary for each in order for them to be useful in a search engine reputation management campaign. The following list of property types and guidelines for optimization can serve as a general blueprint for addressing on-page SEO ranking factors with assets selected for the campaign. As always, when approaching any property or asset, refer to the full overviews of SEO ranking factors provided in other sections of the book.

Many optimization opportunities are consistent across different types of properties, but many also provide unique points of data influence that should be taken advantage of when available. The following data points should be optimized at every opportunity regardless of the type of asset needing optimization.

- Meta Data *(Page titles & descriptions)*
- Heading Tags *(Headlines and sub-headlines)*
- Text Content *(Text information displayed on the page)*
- URL Taxonomy *(Web page addresses and the structure of words in URLs)*
- Contextual Linking *(Links from one page to another, within the text)*
- External Links *(Links pointing out to other resources or documents)*
- Media Content *(Images, video, documents, files)*
- Image File Names *(search-phrase.jpg)*
- Image Alt Text *(Alternative text seen on hover or describing an image)*
- Content Tags *(Defining what a section of content is, article, bio, etc)*
- Breadcrumbs *(Text or links showing a visitors navigation path)*
- Navigation Structure *(Site architecture and relationship between pages)*
- Anchor Text *(Words used in links point to internal or external pages)*

Most of these optimization opportunities take the form of input fields on a given platform or property, and are often not labeled with the SEO factor criteria above. Depending on the property type, users can typically populate the input fields with information, which results in the necessary fields being optimized for search. Depending on the type of property, the access level of the person managing the campaign, and the type of content or media assets being published to a property, some additional unique opportunities for optimization are possible.

In general, any time it is recommended to "optimize" an input field or element, this simply means that it is an opportunity to insert an optimized search phrase for the campaign objective, relevant information about the business or subject, or related details that increase the relevance score of the property being updated.

Optimizing a field or element does not always call for the use of the campaign keyword or target search phrase, in fact, doing so may result in the page exceeding the optimization thresholds that are ideal for a given page. Almost always, it is best to include the primary campaign search phrase in the title/name/heading/description/body text/image & media file names, and a few other places. With these primary fields optimized with the campaign search phrase, other fields offer opportunities to increase semantic relevance and specific details about the business, person, or subject of the reputation campaign.

News & Press Releases

News sites are in essence, editorial in nature, so they typically support a body of text. The text itself should be properly optimized according to the recommendations provided in the "Website Content" sections. Some press release platforms, such as PRWeb.com, BusinessWire.com, or Newswire.net support the optimization of many other variables within the press release, including the title, summary, URL of the page where the release will be published permanently, supporting images, promotional videos, hyperlinks, business contact information, and more.

All fields supported and made available by the PR distribution platform used should be optimized for the target search term and related terms. The title and summary of the press release should include the campaigns primary search phrase (often the person or business name). The title of the press release will become the title of the press release page (meta title) and the content heading within the page. The summary or description becomes the meta description of the page and subtext under the page heading. These are two very important elements to optimize for any press release engineered to be an asset in the reputation campaign.

The content of the press release should use the maximum allowed amount of text characters possible for the PR platform, and should include the max amount of supported hyperlinks to other assets in the campaign. This cross-linking opportunity from press releases provides an opportunity to strengthen other assets in the campaign and create connective relevance between properties that are intended to rank above negative listings. Usually, PR distribution platforms allow for 2-3 links within the text so choose them wisely.

Images and videos are often supported and can be a great way to incorporate rich media into a news release. Using images and videos in press releases is highly recommended.

Among PR distribution services, Newswire.net supports the most on-page optimization opportunities by a long shot. When publishing from this platform, press releases can include all the typical elements of a press release such as title, summary, body text, contact information, images, and videos, and it also supports search engine friendly rich snippets (schema) that help search engines identify more pieces of information about the release topic and the company or organization featured in the story.

For press release strategies, concepts, and more opportunities to leverage PR as a tool in the reputation campaign process, please refer to the section on "Press Release Resources".

Social & Professional Profiles

Social and professional platforms like Facebook, Twitter, Google+, LinkedIn, Pinterest, and CrunchBase are a great resource for developing and optimizing assets in a reputation management campaign, and many unique features are available depending on the specific social site being used by the person or business. Popular social platforms and professional profile sites show up on the scene with tremendous domain authority and are easy to optimize quickly for search placement.

Many social platforms include some or all of the fields listed above, however most people and organizations only populate a small percentage of the fields available. When it comes to using a social profile as a reputation management asset in a suppression campaign, it is vital to populate all fields possible with relevant and accurate information. Be sure not to stuff search phrases or keywords in unnatural places, and make sure the profile is accessible to the public. If the profile is not set to "Public" in the privacy settings, the search engines will not be able to access the page and it will not serve its purpose in the campaign.

Without going into each specific social platform and the differences between each, here is a general list of fields that can be optimized to further increase the relevance scores of a social profile:

- Name
- Username
- Web Address (URL of page)
- Banner/Background Image
- Profile Picture
- Photos/Albums
- Videos/Albums
- About/Bio
- Short Description
- Long Description
- Birth date
- Start Date
- Industries
- Employment
- Education
- Places Lived
- Address
- Phone Number
- Website
- Email
- Interests
- Favorites
- Skills
- Experience
- Life Events
- Mission
- Awards
- Products
- Posts
- Updates
- Articles
- Email

All the on-page optimization recommendations provided in the "Website Content" section apply to any text content published to a social profile page. Also, do not miss the opportunity to consistently publish content to the social profile because social media profiles fall under a special type of ranking criteria related to "freshness" and recency (See: QDD). A social profile without a somewhat steady introduction of new content or updates will likely not sustain its ranking with the search engine because it provides an impression that the page is stale or no longer managed by the owner.

To create a list of possible social and professional sites applicable to the reputation subject, search Google for the current most popular or widely used social and professional sites. Plenty of lists have already been organized (See: Sourcing Links) with certain stats that may be helpful in the selection process.

Guest Editorial Content

Content can often be acquired or published on industry sites or related blogs, in which case the campaign manager or reputation owner would not have direct control over the website or page containing the content. In these cases it is necessary to provide the guest editorial publisher as much of the content and rich media assets as possible, and treat this publication similar to a press release where the content and media assets can be created and sent to the publisher to be posted on the website.

Focus on the title, text, images, videos, and any other content that can be controlled, and depending on the author/publisher relationship, it might not hurt to request further optimizations of the page to increase the relevance of the publication for the campaign search phrase. For example, the person engaging with the publisher could request that the page be optimized in terms of URL taxonomy, Meta Information, Authorship or Content Tags, Image Alt Text, etc. Again, this entirely depends on the publishing platform and the relationship flexibility, but it does not hurt to seek more optimizations where possible

Free Blogs

Blogs and blog content can be created quite easily. All that one needs to do is head over to the nearest free-to-the-public blogging platform with some well-written content, create an account, and start publishing. Many platforms are available for easy blog creation, optimization, and content publishing. Some of the more popular blogging platforms include Blogger, Wordpress, Weebly, Tumblr, and many others that allow free account creation and website setup.

Similar to profile sites, public blogging platforms are typically very large websites with high domain and page authority, so establishing blogs and publishing on these types of properties are a good way to create authoritative assets on sites with a high probability of achieving top rankings in search.

151

Depending on the blogging platform used, a number of features may be available through the blog customization options provided by the website. Most blogging platforms that work well for the reputation management process include the following types of features that should be deployed and populated with relevant content and media assets:

- Blog Title
- Blog Description
- Banner or Background Images
- Logo & Custom Design
- Colors & Backgrounds
- Menus & Link Navigation
- Blog Categories
- Pages of Text
- Posts of Text
- Featured Images
- Location
- Excerpts
- URL Customizations by page
- Widgets
- Search Functions
- Recent Posts
- Archives of Content
- Blogroll Links
- Social Profiles
- Text Boxes
- Blogs I Follow
- Calendars
- Social Share Plugins
- Image Galleries
- RSS Feeds
- Tag Clouds
- And Tons More..
- Search Functions

Blogging platforms provide a convenient level of control over the properties and published content, and provide many unique features that can be deployed to customize the blog assets into meaningful properties for a person or business, while answering to all the optimization factors required for success in a reputation strategy.

Many platforms exist for the purpose of creating a public blog, and many "Free Website" platforms are available such as Wix, About.me, and others. These types of free website platforms often provide a similar amount of deployable customization features, and should also be leveraged in the asset creation and optimization process depending on the needs of the campaign. As it is with all custom properties and websites, following all the SEO ranking factors and on-page optimization criteria is highly recommended.

Video Platforms

Video platforms such as YouTube, Vimeo, and DailyMotion provide excellent opportunities to create custom, media rich, well-optimized profile pages, video channels, and unique video landing pages for SEO rankings and reputation management objectives.

These large, video content heavy websites are some of the most SEO-powerful mega sites available to the public, and they are entirely free (unless you use them for advertising or are a premium subscriber).

Creating an account on these platforms is only a couple clicks and some personal details (accurate and true or not), and one can immediately begin preparing a user profile for a person or business and start the process of optimizing new or existing assets for a reputation campaign.

Video sites have a series of unique features that should be optimized, depending on the specific platform. Similar to social media profile sites, video platforms have a special set of fields and features available that allow profile pages and video channels to be optimized in ways that gain traction quickly in search.

As a rule, take advantage of as many of the fields and features as possible for any given user profile, video channel, or actual video upload. The following are some of the customizable features when using a platform like YouTube.

Video Platform Optimization Elements

Standard Elements
- ◆ Name/Username
- ◆ Custom URL (web address)
- ◆ Banner Image
- ◆ About Description
- ◆ Channel Navigation
- ◆ Related Links
- ◆ Country/Location
- ◆ Video Uploads
- ◆ Video Playlists
- ◆ Featured Channels
- ◆ Discussion Feed
- ◆ User Posts
- ◆ Custom Sections

Custom Sections (channel page)
- ◆ Popular Uploads
- ◆ Uploads
- ◆ Liked Videos
- ◆ Posted Videos
- ◆ Live Now
- ◆ Upcoming Live Streams
- ◆ Past Live Streams
- ◆ Created Playlists
- ◆ Single Playlist
- ◆ Saved Playlists
- ◆ Multiple Playlists
- ◆ Posted Playlists
- ◆ Subscriptions
- ◆ Custom Groupings
- ◆ Recent Activities
- ◆ Recent Posts

Video Uploads
- ◆ Video File Name
- ◆ Video Title
- ◆ Custom Thumbnail Image
- ◆ Video Description (treat this like an article page)
- ◆ Description Hyperlinks (link out to other assets)
- ◆ Tags (insert all relevant/related terms)
- ◆ Captions
- ◆ Transcription (clean this up!)
- ◆ Category of Content
- ◆ Video Location/Language
- ◆ Video Language
- ◆ Recording Date
- ◆ Comments (enable/disable)
- ◆ Syndication Settings (locations)
- ◆ 3D Video categorization

The large selection of widgets and features available on YouTube channels alone present a great opportunity to create engaging, media rich SEO pages that the search engines reward with high relevance and authority scores. These feature sets, deployed with creativity and ingenuity, combined with general SEO guidelines for profile optimization, will provide great advantages in creating and optimizing new and existing assets for SEO and reputation management results.

Image Platforms

Similar to platforms dedicated to video hosting and sharing, websites exist for the purpose of uploading and sharing images. Platforms like Pinterest and Flickr offer users the option to create user accounts, public profiles, boards, collections, and albums of images. These image sharing websites infiltrate search engine image results feeds with photo and image content frequently, as they are the most widely adopted user-generated databases of images anywhere.

The more popular and effective image sharing platforms have been built with search optimization in mind, and much of the technical optimization work has already been taken care of. Leveraging these platforms for search positions and reputation campaigns is just a matter of creating or accessing the user account associated with the asset, and following a few steps to ensure the image profile landing page is optimized properly.

Consistent with other social and video profile pages, make sure that the profile username, name, URL, and description is optimized for the target search term, and take advantage of all the features available for uploading images and creating collections, boards, and albums.

When uploading images, name and describe images according to relevant topics pertaining to the campaign's primary search phrase, and organize these images in boards or collections that are also named and described with relevant topics to the campaign's primary search phrase.

The combinations of uploaded named and described images along with the combinations of image albums and collections result in the needed publicly displaying content and media the search engines analyze when scoring these profile pages. Avoid creating a profile with only a few images or 1-2 collections, as this will not result in a resourceful page the search engines want to serve to its users.

Review Platforms

Many local and national business listing sites like Yelp, and AngiesList offer a consumer review feature that categorize them as "review" sites. These platforms offer the opportunity for businesses to create a local business profile with Name, Address, Photos, Description, Services, Products, and of course, these profiles display reviews.

Many of these platforms offer features that allow the business or brand to populate the profile with relevant details about the organization and their service or products to the public. These sites often fall into the mega-site category and have substantial authority with the search engines. Hence why these sites always seem to appear on the first and second page of search results for a business' searched name.

Because these review sites support consumer reviews, they are often the source of a problem for reputation management campaigns, and should be carefully managed with caution and with the consideration of their true nature and purpose: open forums for the community to post their opinions and reviews.

With this in mind, a reputation campaign manager or owner can make decisions about the appropriateness of such profiles in the scope of reputation risk/opportunity assessment.

Employment/Job Sites

Commonly referred to as "Job" sites, platforms like Glassdoor and Indeed provide businesses opportunities to create company profiles and post available jobs, compensation plans, benefits, and other details about the organization as a means to present themselves to the employment community.

Job sites are typically very large, authoritative websites with hundreds of thousands, if not millions of pages. Staffed with strong IT departments and SEO professionals building the templates that govern the display of pages, business profile pages on employment type websites typically perform very well in search.

Job related website platforms offer many of the typical features of a profile website, but also provide a set of unique features that are exclusive to these unique profiles. On a typical employment website profile like one that might be created on Glassdoor, it is recommended to optimize as many of the following features as possible:

◆ Company Name ◆ Headquarters
◆ Banner/Profile Picture ◆ Founded Date
◆ Overview/About Information ◆ Competitors
◆ Company Photos ◆ Mission
◆ Website URL ◆ Values
◆ Company Size ◆ Jobs
◆ Company Type ◆ Salaries
◆ Industry ◆ Interviews
◆ Revenue ◆ Benefits
◆ Reviews

As it goes with all public facing profile sites, leverage all the opportunities available to populate information to the page. Search engines analyze these pages with considerations of accuracy, relevance, usefulness, and authority, and the more input fields completed with precise information about a business or brand will result in a more optimized page that the search engines determine appropriate to display to users.

Consider that employment profiles have a review feature for current or past employees, so be sure this is an appropriate property to create for a given brand or business and avoid any liabilities that may transpire from having an open forum for people to submit comments to.

Resume Sites

Similar to employment sites, resume type websites (like Resume.com) allow individuals in the employment sector to submit a public resume of work history, skills, accolades, and accomplishments.

Anything that is typically included in a person's resume can also be published to a public facing profile page on a resume site, and the more information about a person that exists on the resume page, the more the search engines score it with relevance for a person's name search.

With rebuilt templates users can populate with information, sites like resume.com allow users to brand themselves in the employment sector by way of resume optimization. Like any website profile, take advantage of all opportunities to include details about the person with the profile, including the name, address, objective, skills, experience, education, hobbies, interests, work history, awards, accomplishments, and any relevant details about the person.

Local Groups

Regional associations, city municipals, and social event groups often provide "local" event type websites where a business or person can create a page about a social event, mixer, or corporate gathering. Websites like Meetup.com provide the opportunity to create a profile page, and an event page that features a specific group or purpose for gathering, with event details, locations, times, attendees, and descriptive information and images about the particular occasion.

With a meetup.com event page, there are many unique features available for optimization of SEO criteria, and these pages are typically very authoritative in search for a business, brand, person, or particular subject and location. Input fields on local groups and event pages should be thoroughly optimized. On meetup.com, an event organizer can populate any number of the following fields and/or the event page is automatically populated with details based on the type of activity the event page achieves:

◆ Name of the Group	◆ Group Reviews
◆ Custom URL	◆ Upcoming Meetups
◆ Background/Graphic	◆ Past Meetups
◆ Custom Logo	◆ Calendar of Events
◆ Description Text	◆ Organizer Names
◆ Location	◆ Contact Information
◆ Founded Date	◆ Sponsors
◆ Attendees List	◆ Headline Copy (page title)
◆ Members	◆ Recent Updates
◆ Photos	◆ What's New (photos/videos)
◆ Discussion	◆ RSVP Updates by Users
◆ Polls	◆ New Member Participation
◆ Files	◆ Related Groups

Like many public facing profile pages on socially influenced/participation websites, the profile pages on meetup.com and local group platforms are often seasoned with more content the longer the page is active and the more events come to pass.

Organizers have the ability to seed these event pages with tons of relevant information about a business or topic for the purpose of optimized asset creation. If creating a local group or event page on a site like Meetup.com, be sure to take advantage of all the opportunities to populate content to the profile, and input details in all available fields for the profile.

Asset type optimizations, in summary...

By following the recommended SEO ranking factors criteria, the general guidelines for profile and asset optimization, by being resourceful, and adding a bit of creativity, it is fairly easy to create powerful new assets or optimize existing properties for the purpose of successful reputation management.

For those looking for a quick and reliable list of websites to create property assets that consistently work well in the reputation management process, here's a proven list of effective sites that are free and easily accessible.

Proven List of Asset Sites

◆ YouTube	◆ Pinterest
◆ LinkedIn	◆ Yelp
◆ Facebook	◆ Manta
◆ Google+	◆ Weblist.me
◆ Meetup	◆ SlideShare
◆ Ask.fm	◆ Aboutus.org
◆ CrunchBase	◆ My.Opera
◆ SeekingAlpha	◆ Soup.io
◆ Mashable	◆ Wordpress
◆ blogs.Forbes	◆ Blogspot
◆ Resume.com	◆ Weebly
◆ Twitter	◆ Tumblr
◆ SoundCloud	◆ Wix
◆ Instagram	◆ About.me
◆ Flickr	◆ Flavors.me

These are just a few of the many available platforms for digital profile creation, optimization, and content publishing. (Find More In: Sourcing Links)

Building Asset Authority

If clarity has yet to be acquired about the way search works and the methodologies search engines use to determine the sort order of results, this is the part of the book that distills the seemingly ambiguous logic process down to actionable insights a person can use to directly influence the position of a property for a given search query.

Provided that the campaign manager or reputation expert has met the necessary on-page SEO ranking criteria with asset creation and optimization, a series of additional tactics may be followed to effectively promote, strengthen, and position campaign assets at the top of search results.

Defining Reality

Search engines must analyze variables on, and off the website or property to determine its relevance and trust within a given search vertical. If the logic behind this methodology and the off-site ranking factor contingencies detailed in the section "Off-page SEO Ranking Factors" have not been thoroughly studied, stop reading this section and revisit that information.

Proceeding through the following sections without a thorough explanation of off-page ranking factors will likely result in confusion and a devaluation of the high-level tactics to follow.

The harsh but helpful reality that needs to be addressed, is that even though a business, person, or reputation manager can create amazing, relevant, information rich, possibly beautiful campaign assets through the steps of property creation and on-page optimization, those properties will not serve the campaign objectives without a diligent approach to inbound, asset strengthening tactics.

Even if the assets and properties are created on a mega-sites like Facebook, YouTube, CrunchBase, or Yelp, and inherit strength through the main domain's authority, the simple existence of a page on one of these sites (even if hyper relevant to the search phrase) does not guarantee, or even suggest the probability of it performing well enough in search to overtake a negative listing in a suppression campaign.

In today's reality of search engine sophistication, in order for a search engine to be "convinced" a new property should overtake results they have already "decided" are the best results to display to users, the property needs a substantial amount of authority signals from external, inbound sources of credibility.

To further challenge the campaign manager, a property asset in an SEO or reputation management campaign will only succeed in overtaking the negative listing if it is A) more relevant and optimized for the given search query, and B) more authoritative than the negative listing. Considering the common "problem" websites and properties that contain negative content are relatively authoritative and trusted (otherwise they would not be positioned at the top), this process of overtaking the authority scores of a negative property can be quite challenging. However, a skilled campaign manager (or determined novice) can follow the steps in coming chapters to quickly outrank negative properties with inbound links and authority signals.

Link Building

Many have said that in the world of SEO strategies and opportunities, "Content is King". If that is true, then inbound links are the soldiers in the army storming the country's castle. True, without quality content and well-optimized properties, links can only do so much for the strategy. Just as an army without a king might go rogue, face misdirection, or be completely ineffective, a king without an army is vulnerable and much less powerful.

The strategy information to follow is the unseen mass of the iceberg under the surface of common SEO strategy; The limitless supply of oxygen for the self-contained underwater breathing apparatus with which a reputation campaign manager can initiate depth charges and swim casual laps around the search vertical iceberg enemy.

Link building, when executed correctly and carefully, has the power to take an otherwise useless, underperforming web property and turn it into a profitable, sustainable digital asset for a business or person. When conducted carelessly or without finesse, link building can do irreversible damage to a property or website, sending it plummeting in search position or possibly resulting in the website becoming penalized or de-indexed in the search engine altogether.

As important as link building is in the success of any SEO or reputation management strategy, it makes sense to acquire a thorough education on the tactics, options, risks, and the rewards. The following may serve this need for the right education.

White Hat vs. Black Hat

SEO techniques are typically classified into two broad categories: white hat and black hat. According to search engines, white hat refers to techniques that search engines recommend as part of their best practice guidelines and are encouraged as low-risk, sustainable methods, whereas black hat tactics seek to exploit loopholes in the search algorithms and rank website's higher than they actually deserve to be positioned. Hmm...

Are not all "SEO" (search engine optimization) strategies designed to increase search position? Do they not all give a person the ability to increase a ranking position higher than was originally rewarded? Seems like search engines are OK with people being somewhat effective at increasing search position, but they are uncomfortable with people being becoming very good at it.

The question that should be asked then, is how can the search engines recommend, "approved" methods but discourage other methods? Well, the answer lies within the effectiveness with which certain tactics have the ability to exploit loopholes in the search algorithms to gain ranking positions. Remember that the primary task of the search engines is to correctly, accurately, and safely answer questions. With vulnerabilities in their ranking algorithm, anyone can manipulate ranking positions by figuring out where the weaknesses are and by implementing tactics to take advantage of them, right?

Yes and no.

Search engines have extremely sophisticated processes and formulas to effectively score and rank pages based on true authority signals, so it is not as easy as learning a little bit about where their weaknesses are and attacking them. Granted, many people (SEO and reputation management experts) make a living at doing this well, and a privileged few have sustained their preeminence in doing so (wink).

Admittedly, the grayscale of SEO best practices can be quite confusing to someone just entering the industry or considering services, and the search companies themselves often create more confusion around the already complicated plethora of options. For example, Google provides a set of Webmaster guidelines and "SEO best practices" which many public Google employees have helped explain to the Webmaster community, then certain Google representatives (who shall remain unnamed for legal concerns) have publicly stated things like, "If you are doing any SEO, it's considered black hat".

Ok...

As mentioned in the ethics chapter, this is not a book that takes any particular hard line on right and wrong in the digital world, but rather aims to provide perspective to those interested in the SEO and reputation management strategies and options available. With that said, this section of this book might intensely challenge rigid ethical stances taken by many in the industry. Furthermore, certain link building tactics have more or less sustainability, more or less effectiveness, more or less risks, more or less difficulty, and require more or less money to execute, so it is worth exploring the tactics and circumstances that may warrant them.

In general, white hat linking might be considered anything that was naturally created, meaning that a website received a link from another website because the linking website had an interest in the content, was a friend of the owner of the website, wanted their audience to see something special at the other website, or posted an image/comment/video from the other website that carried a link to the source website. These types of links are typically considered "organic" or "natural" because they happened by way of a naturally occurring thing.

Many forms of "content marketing" options are available for digital publishers that facilitate the active sharing of content that links back to the originating website source. Publishers who create quality, sharable content are often rewarded by other website owners who republish that content on their website which carries an attribution link back to the source website. Many people in the SEO industry who do take an ethical stance on linking consider this type of link building "ethical" and "white hat" on the grounds that the publisher is providing quality content, so of course it deserves to be posted and shared on other sites. But are we now entering a gray area because these links are being manufactured and "encouraged" by the owner of the website? If you wrap a link building strategy in a pretty "content marketing" bow, does that suddenly make a link building strategy transform from black-hat to white-hat? Where is the line drawn?

Leaping far into the other side of the gray scale, many link building strategies involve the mass production of articles by scraping other websites or generate web page content in bulk from a seed article (article spinning), and the use of automation tools that post those articles into unsuspecting open forums, public article directories or blogs, or independently owned websites. Many link building software solutions are built for the purpose of exploiting open comment fields or profile creations on websites for the purpose of injecting random comments with embedded hyperlinks into them, often resulting in the mass acquisition of links from other websites. Some of these tools have the ability to generate millions of links per day, and thousands per minute. These types of link building tactics and tools may very well be considered "black hat", or less ethical by many in the industry, certainly by search engines.

Link building, as clarified, is essential to boost any property's search position into a secured top ranking, and comes with many challenges for a reputation management campaign. Any reputation management campaign that aims to control the entire 10 results on the first page of the search engine will have to involve a link building component, which often means link building to 10 or more web properties in order to overtake the content that is already there.

Understandably, conducting strategies designed to "game the search engines" (or that follow their best practices?) come with ethical concerns. Fine. But a "white hat" or "ethical" link building strategy that works for boosting the ranking position of 10 (ten) uniquely different properties that need to be strengthened so much that they end up providing control over an entire search vertical is highly unlikely. This requires a whole lot of "quality content marketing" that somehow results in enough links to each of the independent assets in the campaign manager's target list of properties for the campaign. Even the most aggressive of public relations tactics, marketing, and buzz-generation strategies would have a tough time generating the precise amount of inbound authority to all the right target properties.

Enough "naturally" occurring links to the Facebook page of a person with a reputation problem will never be created. The poor wife of the fraudulent CEO who now has a reputation problem is not doing any content marketing. The humiliated student who has been the topic of another student's personal blogging quest is not doing a high-powered public relations strategy. 99% of people with reputation problems do not even have their own website, let alone any groundbreaking informational "content" to share with the world.

Reputation management companies that are not conducting any aggressive linking are simply not performing as well for their clients as those who are. Their ethics, although grounded in convoluted logic, is great? Effectiveness, and their ability to deliver on their promises are severely limited. A graying of white hat "ethics" occurs when a reputation management company promises a client a clean first page in Google, but knows for certain the so-called "white hat" safe linking strategies they are using will never produce the desired, highly priced outcome the client signs up to receive. Of course, it is possible that the reputation management organization or the "experts" behind the company are limited in knowledge and experience and are buying their own misperception (lies) about what works in search and what does not.

The arguments presented here are for the purpose of adding perspective to the industry, educating the consumer of reputation management services about the viability of "safe" options, and of course serve as a primer for learning about the tactics and strategies available.

The following sections will not be labeled as black hat, white hat, gray hat, red hat, blue hat, or any hat, simply because the author does not desire to further smear an already color-confused industry with "ethical" concerns. The person in need of reputation management most often does not care about what the industry or the search engines think is the right or wrong way to do SEO. People and businesses in need of reputation management most often just want a solution that works, and do not want to spend money on one that does not. Each method described in the "Sourcing Links" section will be prefaced with levels of risk and reward, so that appropriate evaluations may be made around which strategies are economically appropriate and viable for a given reputation management campaign.

NoFollow Link Attributes

The "nofollow" link attribute is a value that can be assigned to the rel attribute of an HTML <a> element to instruct some search engines that the hyperlink should not influence the ranking of the link's target in the search engine's index.

Nofollow link attributes are commonly used by webmasters who link to other resources or websites, but do not want to pass page authority to them. Passing page authority can dilute a website's self-contained authority, so the nofollow link attribute is often used between internal pages on a website for the purpose of page rank sculpting, as well as for links pointing from the website to another website.

The overuse of non-nofollow links can often trigger a unnatural link footprint for a property or website, so in order for websites and linking targets to have a natural appearing backlink profile, a combination of regular links (some call these "dofollow" even though there is no defining attribute for them) along with nofollow links are considered normal.

Even though nofollow links are not supposed to pass page authority, according to ranking analysis and inspecting of backlink profiles across top ranking pages, it is clear that nofollow links still have their value in the scope of link building options. In fact, nofollow links are often considered "safe" links among the experts in the industry who do a high volume of linking, so these links can often serve as a great way to control anchor text densities, backlink variations, and supplementary types of links. For example, links from most social platforms are nofollow, but still attribute value in the form of social citations and inbound signals.

To check whether or not a link is a regular (dofollow) or nofollow link, simply visit the page the link is on, view the source code by right clicking and selecting "view source", and find where the link is placed in the code by search the code for an identifiable attribute within the link (ie: "mywebsite.com"). In the <a> tag, the presence of the rel="nofollow" attribute will indicate a nofollow link. Certain browser plugins like the SEOQuake toolbar have settings that automatically highlight nofollow links within a page when activated. The takeaways about nofollow vs. follow links are simply that nofollow links are safer in terms of avoiding penalty concerns for an important website, nofollow links are still followed and indexed by search engines, and nofollow links still have their value in the scope of link building and help to make backlink profiles appear more natural.

Understanding Linking Targets

Linking targets are the pages and properties being linked to in the linking campaign. A linking target should be analyzed with various criteria to determine what types of links are appropriate and effective for the given property. Some domains can receive a high volume of inbound links without risk of manual or algorithmic penalty, and some domains receiving the same amount of links will become compromised.

Additional factors must be considered when linking to a property based on the type of content or information that exists on the page, as well as the backlink history to the page, the keyword density of the page or the linking profile to the page, and other conditional variables.

Domain/Page Authority

The domain and page authority of a website or page targeted for linking, largely determines how many links can be safely and effectively delivered to the page. DA/PA has been described in other sections about inbound linking factors, and should be reviewed when analyzing linking targets.

The higher the domain and page authority of a given property, the stronger and more trusted it is in the discerning eyes of the search engines. Some domains like Facebook, Twitter, Pinterest, LinkedIn, Yelp, Wordpress, Weebly, and others listed in the quick and reliable list provided, have such a large mass of indexed pages, inbound links, and high domain authority that they are what many in the industry refer to as being "white listed" with the search engines, which simply means that they are immune to link spam penalties and manual actions by the Google Webmaster (or Webmaster Console) team.

The white listed domains (and any mega-site properties with high domain authority) can serve as great assets for leverage in the SEO process for reputation management. Using pages and profiles on domains with high domain and page authority provides advantages to ranking new content assets quickly, because of the inherent trust and authority of the domains these pages are on.

Many in the industry also refer to this process as "Parasite SEO" which is a concept by which one can quickly rank for a keyword search phrase by using a page on a powerful website (like HuffingtonPost.com, or ireport.CNN.com). These authority sites are also great in the scheme of link building options because search engines are not going to penalize these websites if they start receiving a massive volume of inbound links. Furthermore these types of sites represent a low risk option for campaign managers to strategically leverage different asset properties in the process of influencing search results, which is a much different scenario than conducting SEO strategies for a primary domain that is a precious asset to a business or person.

Privately owned, low authority, low traffic, or new websites typically need a special type of high-quality-only links that do not present any risk in penalty, algorithmic or otherwise. Websites like Facebook have so much activity, so many sites linking to them, and so much "noise" taking place that pumping a couple thousand new links to a page is just a molecule (not even a drop) in the bucket. It is like a party is already happening, with loud noise and music, and someone drops a glass and its barely heard - the sound of the dropped glass is consumed by the surrounding noise. Whereas if a small website all the sudden receives a large influx of links with no prior linking strategy, no domain authority, no traffic and user activity, it is viewed as an unnatural occurrence and will likely seem like an alarm is going off.

Understanding the differences in domain and page authority of the websites and targets being linked to in the SEO or reputation strategy is important for determining the right type, sequence, velocity, and structure of a backlink profile.

Current Position

The current position of an asset in the reputation management campaign may be an indicator of limiting or contributing factors to that page's performance in search. Often, a website ranked in the top 5 results will indicate strength and authority and a body or collection of content and media that the search engines desire for the search vertical, whereas a webpage ranking on page 2 of the search results may indicate an appropriate position based on the content and elements that are contained within that page.

An example of this might be a negative news article about a person positioned in the 3rd spot on the search results page. This news article has an optimized page title, summary, text body, image, and related links to the topic. On the second page of the search results, there is a person's bio page on a professional site, positioned in the 13th or 14th spot. Even though the person's bio page is more specifically about the person, and represents a more accurate source of information about the person, the page itself might not be considered for top placement for a number of reasons.

The personal bio page in this example may have a number of criteria working against its performance in search. The page may only have 200 words of text versus the 1500 words of text in the negative article. The page may have a high keyword density of 4% (ie: many occurrences of the person's name or too many for the length of text) and Google may be positioning that property on the 2nd page of results due to the over-optimization of the search phrase. The page may be broken or producing errors for users attempting to access that page. Any of these may be a logical reason that the page ranks organically (without influence) on page 2 versus at the top of page 1.

The interesting thing about this example of the relevant bio page on page 2 of search results is that if it violates any of the on-page ranking factor criteria just defined or in other regards, it may be a case where sending links to the page does not help. The page itself must be "compatible" with a top ranking position based on its on-page optimization factors for inbound links and promotions to be able to increase its position for the search phrase.

Be sure to evaluate each target property for top position viability before conducting a costly linking or promotional strategy to the page. Avoid wasting resources and time attempting to rank a page or property which fundamentally has no justifying criteria or reasons it should be ranked above another result, and be sure to analyze the target page for any criteria that suggests it may be suppressed in the results for a good reason (such as too high keyword density).

On-Page Keyword Density

Keyword density is the number one offender in the miscalculation of linking strategies pointing to a page. The density of the target search phrase on the linking target page is a strong determining factor in how well links will work in the ranking process, and also help determine whether or not it is "safe" to link to a page with optimized keyword anchor text.

The Google Penguin algorithm is engineered to detect and penalize link spam situations and the pages they are associated with. One of the ways it calculates whether or not a page should be penalized is by the keyword densities both on the page and in the links pointing to the page. A page that has too many keywords in the content may be suppressed to page 2 of the search results by default. Sending more keyword-optimized links to a page that is already suppressed because of keyword density violations will send it backwards in the ranking results even more.

Alternatively, a page that is ranked highly on page 1 may have a high keyword density, yet the search engine (Google) may still determine this page authoritative on the subject and keep it ranked at the top – however, sending optimized keyword links to this page could send it backwards in ranking position because of an exceeded threshold in on/off page keyword density norms.

Off-Page Anchor Text

The anchor text pointing to a page is a strong determining factor in where the page is positioned in search. Be sure to carefully analyze the keyword density of any page targeted for promotion in the campaign. If the page is under a 1.5% keyword density of the target search phrase, consider it safe to point a variety of keyword-optimized variations of anchor text links to this page.

Follow the criteria outlined in the section "Inbound Link Factors" and "Anchor Text" on the diversification of backlink anchor text. It is never a good idea to send too many optimized anchor text links to a page otherwise there is an invited risk of algorithmically penalizing the page in search – regardless if the page is on a white listed mega-site or a regular small domain.

If the page has a high keyword density of the search phrase (above 2%) it is recommend to only use non-optimized anchor text phrases to link to this page, the safest and most appropriate of which are naked URL variations, domain or brand name terms, generic terms, and random contextually relevant conversational terms.

Always side with caution when using anchor text in backlink strategies. If using any type of content syndication or linking automation tools, be sure to consult with an expert when formulating your keyword lists for hyperlinking, and remember that the more variations of words and phrases linking to a target page the better.

Conditional Variables

Many visible and invisible variables apply to pages that show up in search, some of which can be analyzed and calculated with analysis tools and manual checking, and others that require some discernment by the campaign manager or person executing the strategy.

CTR (click through rate) from search results pages is often a large determining factor in where a result is positioned on the page. In the sections for "On-page SEO Ranking Factors" and "Visitor Behavior" there are some helpful insights into how search engines like Google adjust ranking positions of pages based on "user feedback".

The click through rate on a page in search results is a strong indicator of how desirable the page is for users conducting the search. A high CTR will likely cause a page to rank higher, and a low CTR will often result in a page being suppressed in position.

Analyze the target pages in the asset list and ask the question, "Will users likely click this page?" and "Will this page retain a user's visit?" Pages that do not inspire clicks from search and do not retain visitors from search are not as likely to achieve or sustain a top position for the target search phrase. If a target in the asset list is unlikely to pass this important "visitor behavior" score, consider selecting or creating a different asset for link building efforts.

Sourcing Links

Undoubtedly, by now it has become clear that the link building component to any reputation management campaign intending to suppress a negative property in search is of vital importance.

Knowledge of linking ranking factors is a prerequisite to a successful linking operation, so be sure to study the "Inbound Link Factors" section thoroughly, however knowledge of what to do and what not to do is only powerful if resources are made available to acquire links.

While there are reliable agencies available for sourcing all the links needed for target assets and full campaign management (SwellMarketing.com), there are those who desire to manage link building efforts themselves so the following sections describe types of links, methods to acquire them, and recommendations for each.

Content Marketing Resources

Content marketing is the marketing and business process for creating and distributing relevant and valuable content to attract, acquire, and engage a clearly defined and understood target audience, with the objective of driving profitable customer action.

By definition, content marketing requires the strategy, planning, and development of unique and engaging content about a business or person, with the objective of representing the business or person in a positive light while inspiring engagement, further distribution, and publication.

There are many great resources providing tips on content marketing strategies, audience targeting, value creation, and distribution platforms, but very few of them focus on how well this content will perform in search.

SEO Content – Content for reputation management purposes, among other digital contribution objectives, should always be thought of in terms of how well it will perform in the search engines. Any content marketing strategy can incorporate an SEO focus the moment one decides to engineer the content for not only users, but also search engines.

Determining search phrase relevance, relationships, volume, and competitiveness is an important step in turning any content marketing strategy into an SEO content strategy. For reputation management purposes, it is highly recommended to infuse topical relevance and search phrase optimization into the content creation process, so that the content produced and distributed maintains relevance to campaign objectives.

Content Creation – The creation of content can be as simple as writing an article about a topic, to as complex as creating visual infographics and videos. Many tools exist for content creation to help in the process of visualizing and preparing digital content campaigns, such as KnowledgeVision, Lingospot, Visual.ly, Prezi, and Issuu.

Content Curation – Content can be repurposed, reformatted, re-organized, and republished in unique ways that make an original piece of content a new curated version that maintains the original foundation of information but is presented in a refreshing new format. Content can be curated manually and/or offline, and many digital platforms are available for content curation such as List.ly, Storify, Curata, Magnify, and Echo.

Finding Content Writers – It is not uncommon for a business, person, or reputation manager to need help with the content writing process. Writers can be found on any freelance website according to job postings and precise details or experience, or by accessing any of the dozens of platforms specifically designated for finding content writers such as Scripted, Contently, Skyword, Zerys, and WriterAccess.

Content Promotion & Distribution – Without a method of promotion and distribution, great content is not going to produce any meaningful results. For accessing wide and targeted audiences, leverage any of the well-established companies for content distribution and syndication such as Buffer, Outbrain, Content BLVD, Gravity, or OneSpot.

Content Marketing Analytics – Once content has been distributed across platforms, use tools to track engagement and analyze reach, visibility, engagement, and conversion. Several of the common tools include Webtrends, Act-On, Marketo, and Pardot.

Content Marketing for ORM – Creating amazing content and distributing it far and wide does not guarantee any type of success or results in the reputation management process. Similar to guidelines provided for press release publishing and creating news assets, content marketing is considered a form of editorial and the content you create and distribute should follow the "Website Content" sections guidelines for creating SEO optimized content focused on the search phrase target of the campaign.

Additionally, these content marketing efforts should be considered a link building strategy. Leverage the opportunity to embed hyperlinks to other campaign targets in the asset list to further boost and strengthen the inbound link citations of the properties designated to overtake negative content in search. Content marketing can be a powerful method of link building and asset creation when done with a SEO-centric approach.

Business Listings Resources

Commonly referred to as "business directories" and "local citations", business listing sites are a way to create business profiles on local and national directories. The profiles created on business listing directories carry a link back to the primary website and/or a business citation with the NAP (name, address, phone number) of the business. These business listing profile pages often present themselves as campaign assets and also serve as a way to acquire authoritative links to the main domain of the website, strengthening its brand presence and all associated business/social profiles. Without going into the hundreds of local and national business listing directories and itemizing each one, there are many services available for automatic syndication to available directories. Some reliable services for acquiring business listing citations are Yext, LocalEze, and UBL, or if one spot to manage many locations and access all these services more affordably is preferred, check out Moz.com/local

For national business directory links, many platforms exist for this as well. With plenty of online resources for submitting websites to online directories, it only requires a simple Google or Bing search to pull up a list of online business directories to which one can submit their website. There are paid and free versions of these directories, with the paid versions typically providing the most authority and impact in the scope of directory linking options due to the pay-to-play nature of them. Business.com is a good example of a directory site that is being proactive in the way they allow website owners to submit category specific websites to pages with quality content.

Note that these business directories often allow the person submitting the website to specify a keyword or anchor text phrase for the hyperlink to the website being submitted. The best recommendation for this option is to use the brand or website name, or the domain.com as the anchor text. Creative linkers can customize this directory anchor text further, but the safest thing to do for any privately owned website or small domain property is to use the business/brand/website name.

Blogging Resources

By now the concept of "blogging" should be clearly understood as a means for a business or person to publish any type of editorial content to the web. Blogs can be managed or self-hosted, which simply means that the blogging platform may be a free service to anyone who wishes to create an account and start publishing, or may be self-hosted on a website domain that is solely owned by the publisher or associated party.

Blog platforms can be a great source of quality links to reputation campaign assets if the blog platform, the content, and the links meet certain criteria. Free blog sites like Blogger, Weebly, Wordpress, Tumblr, and many similar widely adopted platforms have high domain authority, allow for total control over content presentation and optimization, and of course allow the formatting of links within content.

Creating hyperlinks within content is as simple as deciding where you want the links to be placed within the text, determining where the links should point to (campaign assets), and formatting the links via the content editing tool or hard coding the links into the HTML with the <a href> tag. As mentioned there are many platforms available for blogging and creating links, here is a handful among the hundreds of options:

- Wordpress
- Weebly
- Tumblr
- InsaneJournal
- LiveJournal
- SquareSpace

- Blogabond
- Blog.com
- Blogger
- Bravenet
- OpenDiary

- Terapad
- EduBlogs
- Xanga
- Zoomshare
- Blogr

ProTip: Use any of these sites for asset creation and/or inbound linking strategies to target properties, and maintain a log of all first tier links to assets so you can point more links at these links to strengthen the truncated link authority metrics described in the "Inbound Link Factors" section.

Guest Blogging Resources

Similar to personal or business blogging, guest blogging is an opportunity to have other bloggers publish content that is provided to them. Gaining access to a blogger community is a great way to leverage the power and influence of other websites in related industries, and can serve as excellent avenues for content marketing, qualified traffic generation, and of course – link building.

Links from related industry websites are some of the best, most qualitative links a campaign manager can get for target website properties, as search engines score links based on the domain & page relevance of the referring link source.

Although acquiring links to reputation management assets require some relationship strategies and careful preparation of acceptable content for the partnering blogger's website, these links can be easily acquired if the right content is presented for the blogger who will be posting it on their site.

Many guest blogging and blogger outreach resources are available to help educate the community on effective strategies for content creation and outreach efforts, along with established networks where guest blogging and blogger outreach is encouraged.

Serious content marketers and link builders may find value in participating in any of the following guest blogging networks:

Guest Blogging Sites

- MyBlogGuest
- GuestBlogIt
- BloggerLinkUp
- BlogSynergy
- Guest Blog Genius
- Guestr
- GroupHigh
- BlogDash
- PostJoin
- Copy for Bylines

Create solid, engaging industry relevant content that is unique, original, and informative, or hire freelance ghostwriters to handle the content creation steps. Optimize the content with relevant search phrases to the campaign primary target, or even the exact primary search phrase.

Use high quality original images to spruce up content, tell stories, answer common questions, and focus on creating a holistic cluster of topic relevance. Embed links to related authority resources (campaign assets) and use appropriate conversational anchor text that makes sense to the reader.

Press Release Resources

Press releases have been a staple in the search marketer's toolbox for years, especially since the major Google algorithm updates of 2011 and 2012 (Panda and Penguin). Bringing higher quality content into favor to promote a safer and better web experience, these updates provided opportunities to capitalize on content marketing and press distribution.

Press releases are evolving and do not carry the authoritative weight they used to, as so many businesses are using them solely as a means of self-promotion, however they remain to be great opportunities to distribute optimized content for search engines and the acquisition of inbound links to campaign assets.

Natural links from multiple, high quality, authoritative outside sources, is one of the biggest benefits of having a press release component to a link building strategy. Additionally, if the steps outlined in the "Asset Type Optimizations" for press releases are followed, these press release pages can often become campaign assets helpful in securing top positions in the target search vertical of the campaign.

Plenty of guides and tips are available online for an education in press release strategies and best practices. Among the most important are making press release content newsworthy, making it a good story (or don't bother), getting to the point quickly, including quotes from industry leaders or team members, optimizing it for search, not being cheap with distribution efforts, not attempting to write it if not an experienced writer, posting the release on the affiliated entity's website, distributing press releases regularly, utilizing traffic analytics tools, and making the press release something that other journalists and editors want to republish.

Many veteran marketers in business and public relations have a unique skill of manufacturing press and motivating media agencies and journalists by influencing the frame of reference with which their business or activities are perceived. In other words, they do not leave anything open to interpretation, but rather they proactively engage in media relationships to spearhead the public opinion and perception of business events, operations, and productions. Establishing relationships with journalists and media companies is a smart, yet extremely under utilized aspect of digital marketing that many website and business owners could be capitalizing on.

For those uninterested in establishing media relationships and communicating stories to journalists, there are many self-publishing options available that allow anyone to distribute "news" digitally. The following are some paid and free resources for distributing PR content:

Best Paid Press Platforms

- ◆ BusinessWire
- ◆ Newswire.com
- ◆ Newswire.net
- ◆ PRNewswire
- ◆ Online PR Media
- ◆ PR.com
- ◆ PressReleaser
- ◆ PRLeap
- ◆ PRWeb
- ◆ PRReach

Free Press Platforms

- PRLog
- PressRelease.com
- 24-7 PressRelease.com
- Afly
- afreego.com
- Betanews
- Biblioscribe
- Business Wire
- GGIdir.com
- ClickPress
- Contactanycelebrity.com
- Directions Magazine
- EboomWebSolutions
- Ecommwire
- Ereleases.com
- Ereleases.org
- Express-Press-Release
- ExtraPR
- Free News Release
- Free PR News (UK)
- Free Press Index
- Free-Press-Release
- HelpaReporterOut.com
- i-newswire.com
- India PRWire
- Loop PR
- Marketwire
- Market Press Release
- Media Syndicate
- MyCompanyPR.com
- Nanotechnology Now
- NewsMediaReleases.com
- Newswire Today
- Online PR Media
- PRMac

- Online PR Media
- OnlyWire
- OpenPR
- Post Free Press Releases
- PR9
- PR Free
- PR-GB.com
- PR-Inside
- PRBuzz
- Press2people
- PressAbout
- PressBox.co.uk
- iPressExposure
- PRMac
- PressMethod
- Press Release Circulation
- Press Release Method
- Press Releases Online (UK)
- Press Release Spider
- PR Log
- PR Urgent
- PRWindow
- PR Zoom
- Pyrabang
- Radio - TV Interview Report
- SanePR
- Tech PR Spider
- The Open Press
- ThomasNet News
- UGA Media (Europe)
- UKPRWire
- Webwire
- PostPressRelease
- iPressExposure
- Ireport.cnn.com

61 Press Release Ideas

- Launch of new website or significant upgrade to existing website
- New company establishment or spin-off
- Company reorganization/Adding new business unit
- Milestone achievements
- Company anniversaries (ie: 50 years in business)
- Office relocation or new venue
- Mergers and acquisitions
- New executives and other personnel changes
- Business rebranding
- Company or Business Unit name change
- Product or Brand name change
- Ownership transfers or new partner
- Adopting corporate social responsibility
- Initial Public Offerings and Stock offerings
- Financial and earnings updates
- Securing business funding from Business Angels or VCs
- Free consultations, samples or trial offers
- Free shipping offer/changes in shipping rates
- Latest contests
- Discounts or vouchers up for grabs
- Social Media Giveaways
- New contests and sweepstakes
- Holiday-related/time-limited sales and promotions
- New features/unique uses for existing products
- Referral rewards
- Reaching your 100th customer
- New data release/study about your market
- Helpful tips or content for customers
- Business or industry trend change
- Winning an industry recognized award
- Release of educational information, eBooks/white papers
- Joint stages or media appearances

- Debunking of common "myths" related to your industry
- Inspirational stories from customers
- Predictions about the economy
- Talks, focus groups, live seminars
- New technology trends affecting your industry
- Watch list or warning alert about certain matter in your industry
- Expert opinion about a topic in your industry
- Releasing of Tips sheets or feature stories
- Your opinion/findings or comments about a trending event
- Creative and Outlandish events
- Important customer interview, story and case studies
- Customer acquisition milestones (100th customer, 500th customer)
- Voluntary work
- Local event or team sponsorships
- Recent charitable contributions
- Inspirational stories
- Internship Program/Placement
- Working for free
- Scheduling of in-person seminars or calls
- Success of events held with event related facts
- Appearance at trade shows or live interviews
- Scheduling and success of Web events
- Event sponsorship or partnership
- Running Webinars
- Filing a lawsuit
- Response to being named in a lawsuit
- Response to accusations against your company or industry
- A natural disaster/killing/threat

Link Acquisitions

Links from other websites can be negotiated, purchased, injected, or outright stolen. There are many ways to acquire links from other websites to a page or property, and sometimes it is effective to conduct backlink research on the competing websites ranking in a search vertical, and sniper the links pointing to them.

Stealing competitor links is an old trick (ethics aside) used by some of the more seasoned SEO professionals that prefer to do the least amount of linking effort possible to achieve top placement in a search space. The process of "stealing" competitor links can mean just that, removing a link entirely or replacing a link from one website to a competitor page by switching it with a new link pointing to a different page controlled by the SEO professional. There are many cases where this is possible and impossible, and can be rather difficult to execute based on the nature of access and relationship with the linking website, but it can be done by a few who make this a practice.

Stealing (acquiring) competitor links can also mean finding websites and pages that link to competitor pages, and acquiring those same links to a different page intended to rank. This is a process of acquiring links on the same pages and sites that link to competitors, but does not necessarily involve the removal or replacement of competitor links. Many hyper-competitive industries are filled with aggressive SEO tacticians that watch other competitor backlink stats to acquire more and more of the same links being developed be people ahead of them in search. Alternatively, a top ranking website owner can watch the backlink strategies of competitors ranking below them in search, and sniper their new links in an effort to remain more authoritative in the vertical.

The process of acquiring links, whether it's a cunning battle against competitors or driven by the general need to create authority links to rank higher, requires education about link value, resourcefulness, and budget to acquire them. The following are some typical metrics used by SEO professionals when evaluating link opportunities.

PR (PageRank) is a common, yet outdated, method of measuring the value of a page or link, and is calculated based on a scale of 0-10. The higher the number, the more authoritative the page. PageRank is a metric calculated by Google, which is a determiner of page value based on the authority and volume of links pointing to it. This score is determined in a number of ways, and has undergone many evolutions (and discontinuations) throughout the years of search engine history, but the original logic that still has some fundamental validity is that a page is as important as the probability of a user finding it by randomly searching the web. That logic is derived from the original "PageRank" patent filed by Larry Page (Co-Founder, Google Inc) called *"Improved Text Searching in Hypertext Systems" (Jan 10, 1997)*.

On October 20th, 2015 – Google filed a new patent titled *"Producing a ranking for pages using distances in a web-link graph"* which strongly suggests some changes to its original PageRank patent. The changes involve determining a score for a document (page) by using a diversified set of seed pages and their distance from the resource document, which is a lot like the concepts developed in the TrustRank approach developed by Stanford and Yahoo several years back. (Bill Slawski)

PageRank (PR) whether recalculated, deprecated, or having any current accuracy, can be determined for any page or website on the Internet by using a PageRank checker. In general, the higher the PR of a website's home page or internal pages where links may be acquired, the more authoritative the links may be from that domain.

Domain Authority (DA), and Page Authority (PA) are calculations of website and page strength by the organization Moz. As described in the section "Inbound Link Factors" these scores indicate a domain or page's authority (essentially, the weight and trust they possess for passing "link juice" to another site). Higher domain and page authority of properties that represent inbound link opportunities present better options for link acquisitions than sites with low domain or page authority.

Domain Age is another variable worth considering when evaluating the authoritativeness of a linking opportunity. The older the domain the link is on, the more trusted that link would be.

Relevance is of great importance when seeking to acquire links from any property for any target. Domain and page relevance typically trump other metrics in the value of a link. A link from an unrelated PR9 would not be considered as valuable as a link from a highly relevant PR5 (usually) based on a concept of "Topic Relevant PageRank", suggesting that relevant sites carry more influence in citation value than non-relevant sites.

Buying links from other websites can be done easily, and there are many "Link Brokers" still in operation. Many of them allow for the evaluation of link purchases prior to payment, and many still provide the industry valuable linking options for those looking to spend a little money for the right type of links. This book will not disclose which of these vendors are best or worst, and will not name them by name due to liability concerns and an appropriate level of respect given what they do.

Many of these link purchasing options involve the selling and leasing of links on high authority, well-known websites, related content posts, privately owned domains, and websites built strictly for the purpose of link acquisition sales. Search engines do not think fondly of link brokers because their entire business operation snuffs the search engine's efforts to combat link manipulation schemes. If special links are desired for a website or reputation management campaign, it should be obvious who to ask (wink).

Industry Influencers

Industry influencers are people, brands, or any entities that have established credibility in an industry with a sustained, active audience. Influencer marketing and outreach strategies have been buzzing around content marketing communities for some time, and many of them are willing to do guest blogging and posting of content provided to them. Some industry influencers also insist on creating post content themselves, as many of them have thousands and in some cases millions of active followers.

Acquiring links and social shares from industry influencers is a new-age strategy that still embodies the old school (lazy linkers) approach to getting the least amount but most effective types of links to a website or page. Links from the websites, blogs, or social media channels of industry influencers can provide a substantial bump in ranking positions and are often worth the time and energy to acquire.

Defining an influencer on a case-by-case basis is appropriate, given their reach and impact on the industry in focus, along with stats about their website, traffic, domain authority, social following, content relevance, and other key metrics that define them as an authority in an industry.

In a recent interview, Kristen Matthews, a world-renowned blogger and outreach marketer at GroupHigh.com states,

"Influencers are different for every brand and every brand's campaign. They should be aligned with your brand contextually, and have loyal followers who trust them. They are individuals who have an audience of quality over quantity, and are people with the ability to attract the right people to your brand. They are authentic in their recommendations and have known credibility in their industry."

GroupHigh.com is a powerful tool that organizes the world's bloggers and content publishers into an easy to use interface and outreach marketing system for managing communications and relationships with industry influencers.

Influencer outreach and marketing can be a powerful weapon in a reputation campaign managers arsenal of tactics, and continues to be effective for business and brand marketing strategies intended to shift industry perceptions while staying ahead of public opinion through the power of industry-credible public relations and content publishing.

Article Syndication

Content marketing, press release strategies, guest blogging, and influencer outreach strategies are some of the more above-board methods for getting article content published on the web. Although there are some syndication solutions available in these types of content publication strategies, a strong majority of the article content being syndicated and published by the SEO community is powered by sophisticated web-based software programs that pull, scrape, build, and push-syndicate article posts to hundreds, sometimes thousands of other websites.

Programmers these days are quite talented with Internet software development, and those that where a marketing hat, and in some cases a (black) SEO hat, have the ability to build software solutions engineered to mass-syndicate article content to other websites on the Internet. These programs, sometimes desktop based and web-based, have the ability to scrape content from news sites, social channels, article directories, and any sites publicly accessible, for the purpose of rebuilding, curating, and "spinning" out new article content in a process that posts different or new versions of articles to more websites.

Certain content management solutions like Wordpress, Drupal, and other website or blogging related software solutions have developer communities who create plugins that can be deployed on a website to push content from the website to external sites, pull content from other websites into the site, or curate content from various sources and either repost on or off the site.

Article marketing software programs with article syndication features often tap into public blogging platforms or private networks of sites, allowing the mass-syndication of article content for link building purposes. Depending on the selected network of posting sites, volumes of account creations, and posting settings configured by the user of the software, these programs have the ability to post thousands of articles per hour, giving the user the ability to engineer complex linking profiles to campaign targets.

Due to the radically objectionable nature of some of these automation solutions, and respect to those who build and use these types of programs, although known and mastered, specific software solutions will not be named. The advanced configuration options and strategies possible with these types of programs deserve an entire book and training course (which exists), so if in need of solutions, training, or fulfillment, there are options and all one needs to do is ask.

Manual article submissions and posting are options as well, and there are many "article directories" available that allow users to create accounts and post content. If conducting any type of article/content publishing for link building purposes, it is always recommended to follow best practices previously described about content creation and linking factors.

When analyzing options for article submissions and posting, it is always a good idea to evaluate the domain strength, and link value of the sites available in order to justify the efforts and resources required to be effective in a linking strategy. Here are some general article directory platforms that allow users to submit article content:

Article Directory Sites

- Article City
- Articles Factory
- Article Snatch
- Evan Carmichael
- Ezine Articles
- iSnare
- LinkedIn
- Pitch Rate
- Promotion World
- Search Warp
- Self Growth
- Topdatum
- Medium

Rich Media Sites

As repeatedly addressed in previous sections, search engines love rich media formats and read, index, and rank various types of them. Many website platforms have been developed for the uploading and sharing of specific types of media content, such as PDF documents, eBooks, presentations, audio files, videos, and images.

Media sharing websites allow users to upload document formats and often allow for backlink opportunities within the document, on the source page the documents are uploaded to, or on the profile page of the user account to where the media files are uploaded. The following are some general lists of media types and platforms available for uploading rich media content and acquiring links to campaign targets. Many of these platforms can also be used as reputation campaign assets with the profile page or media file source page, depending of course on how well the profiles, media files, and pages that host them are optimized.

PDF/eBook Sharing Websites

- fliiby.com
- docs.thinkfree.com
- www.edocr.com
- pdfcast.org
- www.powershow.com
- uploading.com
- www.rapidshare.com
- www.2shared.com
- www.authorstream.com
- www.smashwords.com
- www.4shared.com
- www.wattpad.com
- www.lulu.com
- www.free-ebooks.net
- www.docstoc.com
- www.dropbox.com
- www.slideshare.net
- www.scribd.com
- issuu.com

Presentation Sharing Sites

- SlideShare.net
- Authorstream.com
- Brainshark.com
- Show.Zoho.com
- Powershow.com
- Vcasmo.com
- Slideshow.com
- Scribd.com
- Slideboom.com
- Slideroll.com
- SharedDoc.com
- SlideSnack.com
- PresentationTube.com
- SlideServe.com
- MediaFire.com
- SlideRocket.com
- Box.com
- Docstoc.com
- Slid.es
- SlideWorld.com

Podcasts & MP3 Sharing Sites

- SoundCloud.com
- Last.fm
- Bandcamp.com
- Pandora.com
- Filestube.com
- Mediafire.com
- Box.com
- Reverbnation.com
- Finetune.com
- 4Shared.com
- Depositfiles.com
- 2shared.com
- Sutros.com
- Mobypicture.com
- Yourlisten.com
- Thesixtyone.com
- Hypem.com
- Rapidshare.com
- Hotfile.com
- Uploading.com
- Filefactory.com
- Fileserve.com
- Zippyshare.com

Video Sharing Sites

- Yahoo Video
- Youtube
- Video.qq
- You.video.sina.cn
- Flickr
- Photobucket
- Youku
- Daily Motion
- Rediff
- Rambler
- 4Shared
- Your File Host
- Tudou
- Metacafe
- KU6
- TinyPic
- Cnet TV
- Libero
- Multiply
- Imeem
- Video.web.dec
- Jokeroo
- Crackle
- Vidivodo

- Veoh
- 6.cn
- 56
- Vision.Ameba.jp
- Justin TV
- Break
- Hulu
- Blog TV
- Internet Archive
- WebShots
- Truveo
- Crunchy Roll
- GameTrailers
- Tu TV
- MyVideo.de
- E Snips
- Flurl
- Video.daqi
- Dada
- Stage 6
- Buzz Net
- Magnify.net
- Uume

- Vimeo
- RuTube
- Ustream
- YouTomb
- Smotri
- Ebaums World
- Wat.tv
- Live Video
- Live Leak
- Fixx.tvspielfilm.de
- Vbox 7
- Sevenload
- Funny or Die
- Heavy
- Blip TV
- Current TV
- Dalealplay
- Mania TV
- Clip Fish
- Clip.vn
- Mogulus
- Vod Pod
- Vuze

Image Sharing Sites

- 23
- Animus3
- Art Limited
- DeviantART
- DropShots
- Flickr
- FocalPower
- Fotki
- Fotolog
- Gallery 2
- Gallery
- Humble Voice
- ImageEvent
- Ipernity
- Kodak Gallery
- Koffee Photo
- KoffeePhoto
- Multiply
- My Photo Album
- Panoramio
- PBase
- Phanfare
- Photo.net
- Photobucket
- PhotoSIG
- Photoworks
- Photrade
- Picasa
- Picateers
- PicMe
- Pix.ie
- Pixamo
- RedBubble
- rmbr
- Shutterfly
- Slide
- SmugMug
- Snapfish
- Tabblo
- Walgreens
- Webshots
- Winkflash
- Zenfolio
- Zooomr
- Zoto

Wiki Sites

A wiki website operates on a principle of collaborative trust. The simplest wiki programs allow users to create and edit content. More advanced wikis have a management component that allow a designated person to accept or reject changes. The best-known example of a wiki website is Wikipedia.

Wiki sites present opportunities for SEO people or reputation campaign managers to source industry relevant wiki links by editing or submitting content. Often hosted on .EDU academic sites, and in some cases .GOV government domains, wiki links can be a way to supplement link building efforts with diversification and inbound link contributions from authoritative domains.

Anyone can perform a quick Internet search for a list of public access wiki sites that are community driven, and begin the process of contributing content and links. Most SEO people using wikis as a form of link building are not focused on the "quality content" approach and use these types of sites for mass inbound link citations, however some wiki related linking opportunities are well-managed sites with strong community moderation and a link from one of these types of sites can be a strong linking contribution to a target property.

Many automated content posting software solutions exploit the open permissions on wiki sites for mass posting of article content and link injections. Some SEO experts know how to leverage these types of linking tools with wiki posting features for complex, multiple tiered linking campaigns for the large volume citation value and indexing potential they offer, however most people spin and post junk content to wikis with little or no effectiveness in a ranking strategy.

Forum Links

Forums are another form of community driven, user-generated content platforms, typically centered on an industry topic, specific business, or area of research or study. Linking websites and resources within forum threads is a common natural mechanism of sharing information between users, and these types of links are often used for SEO purposes.

Forums typically require a user to create an account, which then allows for the creation of a profile where the user can specify details, interests, profile picture, and a website link.

Forum posts, comments, and profiles have been a large source of linking opportunities for people needing to acquire links to SEO targets or reputation campaign assets, and are best acquired through high quality forums with topical relevance to the focus industry. Links can be created manually or in mass quantities through automated software solutions, which have the ability to powerfully improve or damage a web property's position in search.

Among the many linking types and processes available to people trying to manipulate search rankings, forum profile links have been one that certain search engines like Google flag as unnaturally occurring links. This link value demotion process in forum profile links is always calculated based on the link-receiving site's backlink history and the general likelihood of the particular site receiving those types of links, so it's important to approach these forum linking opportunities with extreme caution if linking to a new or low authority website.

These risks are not present when linking to authority site profiles like Facebook or Twitter, as many users of forums often connect their social profiles on their forum profile page, so in the reputation management process, many campaign targets can safely receive a heavy influx of forum related links.

Many automated forum profile and post creation software solutions exist for the purpose of mass-generating links, and can prove to be useful in sending a high volume of link citations to white listed domains (See: Defining Reality).

With any type of linking, especially with automated solutions that create bulk quantities of links very quickly, it is vital to manage anchor text densities and maintain a natural occurring backlink profile.

Blog Comments

Commenting on posted content is a regular, possibly very familiar activity to many consuming content online. Links can often be embedded into comments on blog posts, allowing SEO professionals to create link citations on industry related (or unrelated) websites that point to campaign targets.

There are many methods for creating blog comment links on other websites, ranging from researching authority sites in related industries and manually creating quality contributions to posts, to the mass injections of comments through large lists of scraped sites that are targeted for comment posting.

The best blog comment link is always going to be the one that occurs on a relevant post, on a relevant and trusted website, on a page that receives traffic or has high authority in search, is a well written contribution, and contains an appropriate link to another related resource. These types of links are valuable in the SEO ranking process of targets in a campaign.

Many software solutions are available for mass injection of blog comments, and each method comes with its risks and benefits. Like other automated forms of linking, a massive amount of blog comment links can be created quickly, and they will either benefit the target or compromise its performance in search position.

Anchor text variation is always important for this type of linking, and should be managed very carefully. Industry relevance and blog domain authority are important in ensuring that these types of links pass value to the linked target. These types of links can damage small, new, or low traffic websites, and can also help them depending on the rate at which they are created and the method by which they are acquired.

Large authority sites immune to search penalties can safely receive a large quantity of blog comment links without penalization, but linking factor criteria should still be taken into account for maximum effectiveness.

Tiered Linking Strategies

Authority links can be difficult to acquire. Content marketing often does not produce the needed boost in rankings for target assets in a linking campaign. Manually created or purchased links often only send a small amount of value to the target page. Automated software solutions produce large quantities of links but typically create pages and links on pages with low authority, resulting in a low link value to the campaign target.

In the section "Inbound Link Factors" and "Tiered Strategies" it was mentioned that link value is often truncated, meaning that the search engines discount the value of a first layer of links and factor in the value those links have based on how many links point to them.

Tiered linking strategies are engineered to pass link authority to links pointing to campaign properties, and can be very effective in boosting the trust and weight of a first layer of links. Tiered linking strategies are also a great way to avoid primary domain penalties, as they serve as a method of cloaking linking strategies with a safe first layer of links, while performing tactical linking strategies on 2nd and 3rd layers of linking tiers.

To describe a tiered linking strategy in simple terms, a campaign manager may publish a press release or public blog post that points a link to a campaign target, then conducts a linking strategy to the press release or blog post, sending link authority to the press release or blog post that links to the target. Layering links in this fashion strengthens the authority of the first tier press release or blog post, which reinforce the value of the link that points to the campaign target from that page.

Due to the nature of tiered linking strategies requiring a typical high volume of links to be effective, tiered strategies are most commonly executed by people using automated software solutions to build lots of links on 2nd and 3rd level tiers. Some industry professionals spend a substantial amount of time and resources on the engineering of tiered campaign strategies to bypass link pattern detection and maintain their ability in successfully avoiding backlink footprints the search engines can easily detect.

Effective tiered linking strategies are reserved for a few skilled professionals in the industry, which often involve a leveraging a combination of public websites, blogs, forums, wikis, rich media sharing sites, press release distribution platforms, directories, and privately owned blog networks built for the purpose of linking.

If conducting a tiered linking strategy, it is recommended to consult with an expert with experience in this type of practice. Without experience and well-established resources, a strong knowledge of backlink ranking factor criteria, and a long history of testing different strategies, and proof of concept, engaging in these types of strategies may result in wasted efforts, lost money, and damage campaign properties.

To try out a tiered linking strategy manually, one could practice linking to pages and properties that link to campaign assets, which has its value if enough links can be resourcefully acquired. If the resources are not available to produce a high volume of authority links, then it is probably best to build links directly to campaign targets.

Please see Done For Your Services for assistance with linking.

Automation Tools

Software automation in the link building process can be perceived as a blessing to those with experience, and a curse to those without the proper training. Automated link building processes provide experienced campaign managers the ability to generate a substantial amount of links in a short period of time, from a variety of different sources, pointing to any desired campaign target, with any preferred sequence, velocity, tiered structure, anchor text diversity, content strategy, or method of delivery. Specific tools and solutions will not be named, nor will the exact campaign strategies or configurations be described. It should be clear that these types of solutions are not recommended by search engine companies due to their cunning ability to exploit ranking factor loopholes and impact-ability on search position manipulation.

Search engines like Google actively attempt to formulate algorithms to combat the powerful influence these types of solutions have on search ranking manipulation, so the tactics and strategies required to be effective can be a moving target – meaning that the SEO professionals that use these methods must remain quick on their feet, adjust strategies constantly, and stay ahead of what the search engines are actively trying to stop. Content quality, uniqueness, and relevance remain to be of extreme importance, along with the website sources, sequences of links, velocity, tiered mechanics, and media/content types used for the generation of links.

Among all automated linking considerations, anchor text diversity is most important when doing any type of automation, article syndication, mass posting, or system generated linking, as it is a ranking factor that can quickly fall off the rails and become difficult to recover. Be cautious of anyone offering these types of links to an important business property, and make sure they follow linking factor ranking criteria carefully. Experienced tacticians in the SEO and reputation management industry use linking automation programs to swiftly control search results pages. These tools and processes maintain a high level of effectiveness when used correctly.

Asset Link Reciprocity

Linking reciprocity between campaign targets is a great way to cross-pollinate authority between properties in search. Search engines analyze the quality, relevance, authority, and "distance and relevance of reciprocating nodes" to determine a page's position in search.

If a campaign manager has 10 properties selected for the campaign, linking between these properties from one property to another is recommended to increase the "resourcefulness" of each property in the vertical. While it is also recommended to link out to other authoritative (non-negative, non-competitor) resources in the industry, it is also a good idea to pass authority between campaign assets through hyperlinks.

Blogs, social profiles, press releases, and just about any type of asset that can be created or optimized provides opportunities for embedding links in content, about or description text, or through profile updates. Reciprocating link value between properties in a reputation campaign sends signals to search engines that pages are related and strengthens their independent relevance for the search phrase target of the campaign.

In previous chapters about "Creating Campaign Assets" it was mentioned that there are some exceptions to this recommendation, which will be repeated here due to its opportunity value and the importance of risk mitigation. The exception to this cross-linking recommendation is if the campaign manager decides to create independent websites on registered domains as a method of asset creation. An example of this might be "mydomain.com", "mycompanydomain.com", and "mycompanyreviews.com".

If all three of these sites in this example are designed and developed for the purpose of ranking for the same search term, they can be linked to and from other properties (like social channels and press releases) but be sure to avoid linking between them. (See: Creating New Assets)

Link Analysis & Monitoring

Inbound links and citations from credible sources are so important for the successful ranking of campaign assets, and there are so many factors involved in a properly executed linking campaign, it makes sense to monitor and analyze the progression of link acquisitions to each target using analytics tools. Link monitoring options range from Google supported webmaster consoles to independent 3rd party link data aggregators, and each are different and provide a unique perspective on backlink profiles for a given property.

Link Analysis Tools

The most common link analysis tools are the ones that provide the highest volume of data and the best analysis of the total links pointing to a page, along with helpful SEO-centric perspectives on the backlinks and sources themselves. Here are the best tools used today for backlink analysis.

- Moz – Open Site Explorer
- Majestic SEO
- Ahrefs

These tools provide the most valuable insights pertaining to backlinks when managing a linking campaign to target properties. Measuring everything from the domain and page authority or trust flow of linking sources, to the topical relevance, anchor text, follow attributes, velocity, and total volume of links, these tools provide excellent insights to the effectiveness of inbound links.

Competitor backlink research is a common practice of professionals in the industry, and is highly recommended for gauging the competitiveness of a search vertical. These tools provide analysis on a domain level and page level, and provide detailed backlink stats on any unique website URL queried for analysis.

Other tools like the Google Webmaster Console allow website owners using the console to review link sources that Google decides to display, and may provide additional information about a website's backlink profile. Due to the nature of this tool and Google's typical practice of revealing only a partial amount of their total SEO data on a website, this tool and the data that it provides on link stats for a domain should not be viewed as the final authoritative source on backlink metrics.

Incorporating this data set perspective might be helpful while using additional tools like Moz and Majestic, but should not be viewed as the entire picture of the linking taking place for a domain or page. In reputation management, it is important to use other tools primarily because it is impossible to see console data on a website that is not owned and controlled by the campaign manager.

Among the many inbound linking factors that should be monitored, there are a few areas of heightened importance when monitoring backlinks. The following sections describe certain metrics that should be watched closely, and the adjustments that should be made based on the data collected.

Monitoring Link Sources

As described in great detail through previous chapters, link sources are an important factor in a linking strategy. The referring domain authority, page authority, and domain/page relevance, should be monitored to ensure that the linking sources are both authoritative and relevant to the target property in the linking campaign.

In tools like the Moz Open Site Explorer and Majestic, each referring domain and linking page will contain authority related metrics associated with the property sending the link to a target. In Moz, these scores are referred to as Domain Authority (DA), Page Authority (PA) and a few other indicators of relevance. In Majestic, these calculations are Trust Flow, a metric of referring domain trust, and Citation Flow, which is a measure of citation volume (or popularity based on links). The tools differ slightly in their calculations as they both have proprietary algorithms for calculating these values, so it is appropriate to analyze backlinks in the different tools to achieve a more holistic view of links to a property.

Ensure that linking targets are receiving a reasonable amount of links from referring sites and pages with authority and trust, which is an indicator of a progressive and effective linking campaign. As the volume of links from authority sites to a target increases, the authority and trust of the target page will also increase. The pages (URLs) analyzed in each tool will also be analyzed in terms of DA, PA, Trust Flow, and Citation Flow, which are scores derived from the inbound links and referring sources. High scores for campaign assets translate to a higher likelihood of these targets performing well in search.

Monitoring Link Velocity

Among other metrics like link volume, authority, relevance, and type, link velocity is a very important statistic to monitor for campaign assets In a reputation management strategy. Link velocity, described in detail in previous chapters, is crucial for ensuring a "convincing" level of growing popularity for the campaign target.

Link velocity is best analyzed in tools like Majestic or Ahrefs, which shows a trend graph for both newly acquired links and disappearing links, indicating how frequently targets are being linked, or how rapidly targets are losing links. Maintaining a positive link velocity is critical, so make sure that the link graphs are trending upward, and exceeding the rate of disappearance or deletion of links.

Referring link velocity is different than referring domain velocity. The analytics tools can be configured to display referring domain graphs and velocity metrics so that a campaign manager can ensure there is a positive trend in referring domains, not just links. A target can be receiving a steady influx of new links, but if all from the same website or source, this will do little to convince the search engines of its increased importance. Referring domain velocity should be monitored for growth.

Monitoring link velocity is a great way to determine whether or not a linking strategy is working properly. Content marketing strategies and outsourced linking providers can often be deceiving in the true linking values they provide in a campaign. Press releases often have limited distribution or actually none at all, and automated software programs can be configured incorrectly or point to the wrong sources. Checking each campaign target in the link analysis tools is a great way to ensure linking campaigns are being executed properly and producing a positive link velocity to targets.

Monitoring Anchor Text

Inbound link anchor text is probably the most important metric to monitor in a campaign target's backlink stats. Refer to the "Inbound Link Ranking Factors" section on anchor text and learn as much as possible about anchor text variables that impact ranking positions. Anchor text can be monitored through Majestic or Ahrefs, and should be checked regularly to ensure an appropriate diversification of text linking to target pages.

As described in the ranking factors section, a campaign target should have a balance of naked URLs, branded terms, keywords, generic phrases, and a wide range of anchor text variations pointing to the page. In general, the most dominant text that should be linking to a page is the brand name, or naked URL variations of the page. Appropriate secondary priorities in anchor text are variations of target search phrases or keywords, then a wide array of related phrases and generic terms.

Majestic and Ahrefs allow you to analyze the anchor text stats of any campaign target URL, to determine the densities of anchor text words pointing to the target. Typically, these stats are displayed according to the most used to the least used, with counts for the number of times the particular text has been used in descending order based on the total number of referring domains using that text to link to a target.

Linking Adjustments

The proactive monitoring backlinks allows a campaign manager to make adjustments in the linking strategy to ensure effective links are being created and the right factors are being taken into consideration. An entire book could be and should be written on the subject of linking strategies and all the necessary adjustments that can be made to ensure a campaign stays on the right track, however the following are the most important areas of focus when monitoring backlinks.

Link sources should be monitored for authority and relevance. If backlinks to a property appear to be low authority, irrelevant, from different countries, or from pages that have little authority or link value, the linking strategy should be adjusted to include higher quality sources of links that pass more value to the campaign targets.

Positive link velocity to targets in the campaign should be maintained and consistently tracked to ensure a steady increase of links rather that a trend indicating a consistent or dominant decrease in links. Adjusting linking strategies and sources may allow a campaign manager to control the inbound link velocity of a target property. One strategy might not produce the needed link velocity, and another may be required to generate the volume of links needed to increase positions. If a property is not increasing in ranking position, and all other factors of on-page and off-page optimization are controlled, low link velocity may be the reason the page is not performing or increasing in position.

Anchor text should be monitored and adjustments should be made consistently to ensure the safe and natural diversification of inbound link text. If a target shows dominance in a particular anchor text phrase, the target may begin moving backwards in ranking position for that phrase, and/or may represent an at-risk linking target that will soon require a de-optimization (or dilution) of anchor text to move it back into a positive ranking position trajectory. Anchor text is often the source of undesired movement of a campaign target in the wrong direction, which could be the result of the page having too high of a keyword density on the page itself and an unnatural threshold being exceeded with off-page anchor text keywords, or just an unnatural amount of inbound keyword links.

Learning about backlink statistics, trends, and objectives based on real-time analysis of links and ranking positions is highly recommended for anyone doing professional SEO and reputation management, and should be a regular practice of anyone conducting a temporary or permanent campaign. The ability to make real-time adjustments in linking strategies is a virtue possessed by any legitimate SEO professional or reputation management expert.

For training, exclusive linking resources, and proven models for reputation campaigns, please see section: Reputation Black Box

Creating Social Signals

Social signals are events that take place on social media platforms relating to a website or domain, often in the form of Facebook shares of a page, Tweets of a URL, Pinterest pins of images from a page, and Google+ post updates that include links to pages.

Importance

Social signals serve as "social proof" of a domain or page's relevance and authority in the Internet landscape, and can provide the search engines valuable data on a property's real-time value, which is derived from socially influenced activity and behavior on social media sites. These activity signals from people on social platforms help the search engines validate the popularity of a web property, and can prove to be very useful for campaign managers conducting linking strategies, because a property receiving a high volume of links but no social signals is not common and usually results in inbound links being much less effective.

Timing

Social media activity is stored in a supplementary search engine index, and helps the search engines better sort search results based on the recency and trend of activity for a property. Social signals that were created several months back do not impact the rankings of a property as effectively as social signals detected within the previous two weeks.

The timing of social signals should correlate with the timing of inbound links to a page in order to appear natural, and may even naturally precede inbound links to a property. Both social signals and links are best delivered to a page that was recently created or updated, which validates the new increasing volume of citations pointing to the page (user activity suggesting "there's something new here").

The timing of social signals can be executed immediately before or during a linking strategy, forcing the search engines to acknowledge a page's importance based on social proof. The same effect can be created with press releases, inherently bypassing link validation algorithms designed to discount the importance of incoming links to a page.

Sourcing Social Signals

Sourcing signals can be done in a variety of different methods, ranging from marketing tactics encouraging friends and customers to share a page to their friends, post a product to their social feed, tweet if they liked a video, and other typical mechanisms of sharing content on social media. There are many educational resources available describing the best practices for getting website visitors to share a page or piece of content on social media, most of which are outright ineffective for a reputation management campaign.

Remembering that the campaign's success hinges on the effectiveness with which many assets and properties are promoted simultaneously for the purpose of gaining top positions, it is highly unlikely that a campaign manager (even if the most savvy in digital marketing tactics) will be able to effectively create enough organic inbound social signals to all the properties within the campaign.

Social signals can also be optimized for greater effectiveness in the ranking process. The text used in the comment area, the images or links shared, and the platforms they are shared on, can all be optimized for better relevance scores. The following describes the best practices for generating optimized social media shares and posts on the most important social signals sources for ranking target properties, along with some methods that can be used to mass-generate safe social signals to a property inside automated software solutions.

Facebook Signals

Shares of a page, reshares, likes, and comments, are the primary signals considered by search engines for Facebook. When a page is shared on Facebook, the post has a set of variables that are automatically generated and some that can be optimized. The automatically populated elements are the linked title of the page, the meta description of the page, and the video or selectable image from the page, and the page source URL. The elements that should be optimized are the post description, a custom image if applicable, additional links, and hashtags.

The description in a Facebook share is a great opportunity to create post relevance for the page being shared, especially within the first 35 and 160 characters of the post. Include the primary search phrase keyword objective for the target page within the first few words of text, as this area becomes the page title and meta description for the post (yes, each post get's a unique page). Use a 615x300 Image if applicable, and implement keyword rich hashtags to increase relevance for the post. Also lengthen the length of text included in the post/share, as this is treated like the body of text on a page. Make sure the post settings are set to "Public" which allows the search engines to read the post without being logged into a user account.

Posts like this can be reshared, liked, commented on, and all activity and engagement of a post including a link to a page sends social signals to the page that is linked. Collectively, all activity on Facebook that can be linked to a unique "page" on the web is the total sum of "Facebook Signals" to that page. Top ranking pages in search typically have a high volume of Facebook Signals.

Twitter Signals

Tweets, retweets, and replies are all signals from Twitter that can help determine a page's relevance and authority in search. Like Facebook shares, tweets should be optimized in terms of text, hashtags, and images where possible. The more uniqueness created with each tweet associated to a page the better, as this results in a unique social contribution by users who want to share that page on Twitter.

The first few words of the Tweet text should be optimized with campaign keyword search phrases and concluding hashtags to indicate relevance and increase the probability of the tweet being displayed in the feeds of other users. As a tweet of a page receives retweets, and replies, more social signals are attributed to the original page that was tweeted.

Top ranking pages in search typically have a high volume of Twitter Signals associated with the pages, indicating that users who have visited that page also shared it with their audience on Twitter.

Google+ Signals

The recommendations and criteria for Google+ closely match those of Facebook, as the platform was built with many of the same features and functions provided on Facebook. A page shared on Google+ sends signals to the page, by way of any activity that takes place on that post/share. All +1's, reshares, and comments on the post that links a page are attributed back to the page that is linked. The more Google+ signals associated with a web page, the more social authority it has, which results in a stronger score for search rankings.

Google+ posts should be optimized with descriptive, search phrase optimized text, images, hashtags, and related links. Unique and original comment text is recommended, along with increased length, the incorporation of hashtags, related links, and images where possible.

Top ranking pages in search typically have a high volume of Google+ Signals associated with the pages, indicating that users who have visited that page also shared it with their audience on Google+.

Pinterest Signals

Pinterest is similar to other platforms except that it is primarily used for the sharing of images and videos. From the page property, an image can be "Pinned" to a Pinterest account, and on the "Pin" page there are several elements that send value to the page from which the image was sourced.

The URL of the page will be linked from the image source URL, the comment area will be the optimized text that also populates the page title and meta description of the page, and comments and repins and favorites can be applied to the pin from other users on Pinterest. All activity on the pinned image, including favorites, repins, and comments attribute positive social signals back to the image source page.

The image source page is the campaign asset being promoted, and more Pinterest Signals result in a higher social authority score for the given page. Top ranking pages In search typically have a high volume of Pinterest Signals associated with the pages, indicating that users who have visited that page also shared It with their audience on Pinterest.

Social Signal Automation Tools

A campaign manager with the task of promoting a handful of unique campaign properties may face a few obstacles achieving adequate social signals for each property, let alone one of them. Because of the level of difficulty in volume necessities and scale, few people in the SEO and reputation management industry leverage the power of social signals with much effectiveness, if they even attempt to incorporate them into strategy.

Those who do run the extra mile to ensure their campaigns and clients maximize results, often use automation tools or outsourced resources to generated volumes of automated or scheduled social signals to campaign properties. Many resources exist for purchasing social signals, which can be accessed by using freelancer "gigs" platforms where social signals can be bought and sold, automated software programs that support mass social profile account creations and schedule postings, and other resources for outsourcing this type of work. Specific platforms and software programs shall not be named due to the nature of ranking manipulation and social signal leverage these programs are engineered to achieve, however they can be easily researched and sourced.

If performing any type of automated social signal generation for the purpose of search ranking manipulation, there are a few rules one must follow to ensure effectiveness and avoid detectable footprints.

Mass posts and tweets are ok, but not the same exact post text over and over on different accounts. Posts by different users/accounts should always be uniquely written, unless the post or tweet is repurposed by other users in the form of a repost, reshare, repin, or retweet.

Avoid creating a massive amount of signals from underdeveloped user accounts that are obviously non-authoritative or fake. These types of signals will do little if anything for the search ranking objective, or worse may discourage the search engines from valuing this page at all.

Monitoring Social Signals

There are many tools available for monitoring the social share and signal history of a page or property. Monitoring social activity of a campaign property will allow the reputation manager to track social signal campaign trends and effectiveness, and will present opportunities to make adjustments in the timing, velocity, and quality of social citations.

Tools can be discovered through a little research, but the Ahrefs link analysis tool and the Moz Open Site Explorer both have social signal measurements for analyzed URLs. Additional social signal monitoring tools can be useful, such as ShareTally.co or SharedCount.com, which allow any public user to insert a URL and check the total counts of social metrics from different platforms.

Creating Brand Recognition

Brand authority and visibility is of growing importance in the search landscape, and is a mechanism of ranking manipulation reputation campaign managers can employ within the overall strategy. Refer to the sections "Off-Page SEO Ranking Factors" and "Brand Visibility" to refresh or learn more about how these factors contribute to top rankings for a website.

The interesting thing about acquiring brand recognition is all other profiles and pages associated with an authoritative, recognized brand also grow in authority.

Brand authority can be strengthened in variety of ways, so if the reputation campaign objective pertains to a business (or individual that could be a "brand") be sure to follow the proceeding steps to verify and strengthen the authority and visibility of the brand name.

Google+ Brands

Go to https://www.google.com/+/brands/ and each of the steps in the 5 modules of making a brand social. The steps involve:

- ◆ Creating a Google+ Page
- ◆ Complete a profile
- ◆ Verify the page, and claiming a vanity URL
- ◆ Adding the Google+ badge to the website
- ◆ Linking a YouTube channel to Google+ page

Configuring Asset Relationships

Asset linking reciprocity is important, especially when it comes to connecting social profile pages to a brand's website through linking or hyperlinked icons. This process of configuring asset relationships for branding is primarily designed to make sure there are proper linking connections between a brand's social and professional profiles and with the website. Leverage every opportunity to interlink all social/profile pages with other social/profile pages. There are often preconfigured fields for linking a "Facebook URL" or "Twitter Account" so use these where possible, or seek to embed hyperlinks to other social profile pages within the About or Description text areas of profiles.

Create Business Listings

Follow the steps outlined in the "Sourcing Links" and "Business Listings" sections to create business citations for a brand, as doing so will increase brand relevance and create more address citation history for the official business name and address, which strengthens a business' authority with the search engines.

Business listing directories are often authoritative, local, industry relevant sources that "reference" a business according to its official information. If no public storefront or office location is available or desired by the business, there are cases where a virtual office address or PO Box address may be used in place of a street address. Use the Moz.com/local service, LocalEze, or Yext service to deploy a convenient citation campaign for a brand.

Maintain Active Social Presence

Keep social profiles and accounts fresh with recent content and updates. The more frequent and recent the content present on social and professional profile sites the better. More frequent content and posts on these channels results in a higher freshness score and recency metrics benefit brands desiring higher placement and prominence in search results.

Active social accounts suggest the brand is engaged with its community of followers if it is frequently providing updates to its fans. Even if no followers exist on the social property for the brand, maintaining an active social presence through posting content will benefit the ranking strategy of campaign assets and brand importance.

Publish Content

Brands and businesses that publish regular useful content become more recognized for industry relevance and importance than those that do not. Content publishing is best done on the website itself, but could possibly exist on an associated blog. However or wherever the content is originally posted by the brand, it should be reposted and shared to the brand's Google+ page and other social channels as a mechanism of content publishing that convinces Google it is actively engaging its audience with a brand presence.

Get Business Reviews

Consumer business reviews help reinforce a brand's recognition and can be acquired through many sources where the business has a public profile with review features for users. The more reviews a brand acquires the more importance the brand is rewarded. Importance in this context does not necessarily indicate quality or anything good, so if "reviews" are a liability in a reputation management campaign, proceed with caution because more reviews will result in a more prominent position in search for any profile receiving the reviews.

Positive reviews strengthen brand prominence as well, and can serve as a valuable asset in the brand recognition process. Reviews on Google+ or Yelp might be the most obvious places reviews can be acquired, but again, proceed with caution because they present the public an opportunity to share their opinion.

Navigational Searches

User demand for a brand or specific pages on a website can serve as a signal to the search engines that the community desires a specific brand. These navigational searches are in essence a search for any brand, business, website, or page on a specific website.

Navigation searches strengthen a brand's prominence and authority in search and can result in the brand's associated profiles or website pages achieving higher placement in ranking results for brand related and generic industry related search terms.

Searches for a brand might be generated through natural byproducts of popularity and demand, and there are methods for artificially generating navigational searches through crowd sourcing type platforms that allow users to create cheap paid jobs for conducting small actions on the web. These crowd sourcing platforms can be setup with small repeatable search-and-click jobs that freelancers can perform for a small fee, and the more these actions are taken in the search engine, the more a brand might be recognized for its user generated demand signals. The full scope and technicality of creating these types of community generated searches is highly complex and require certain criteria to be met in order to be effective, but its worth mentioning because it is a coveted strategy used by only the most elite in the industry.

In conclusion, brand recognition in search can have strong impacts on a business or person's authority in competitive search verticals, so these branding hacks can be used for both reputation management and regular SEO strategies with great effectiveness.

Image Reputation Management

Reputation management campaigns are often centered on negative images that need to be removed or suppressed, and much can be done to create a more positive image presence in the search engines.

Images fall under a special type of optimization criteria, as they are a unique type of rich media that are sorted and served in a dedicated search portal on search engines. Occasionally, images can creep into regular web search results and cause problems for brands and individuals, which calls for a unique image suppression campaign that can be an intertwined component to a reputation strategy.

Similar to web pages and asset properties, images have their own set of ranking factors that need to be addressed in order to successfully optimize and rank new or existing images for the purpose of suppressing negative images.

Image Search Ranking Factors

According to multiple image ranking algorithms described in patents filed by major search engines Google, Bing and Yahoo, there are specific measurable variables used to score and rank images according to relevance and authority. The following are a common, yet advanced, tested and proven set of image ranking factors one can follow to ensure top placement for image media in image search.

- ◆ Optimized Image Name (Search-phrase.jpg)
- ◆ Domain Name
  - ▪ *Website where the image is hosted*
- ◆ URL, Title, and Meta Data of Page
  - ▪ *Where the image is visible*
- ◆ Text Surrounding the Image
  - ▪ *Weighting words closest to the image*
- ◆ Text Associated With Image on Different Pages
  - ▪ *References, descriptive links to image*
- ◆ Inbound Links to the URL of the Image
- ◆ Embeds of Image on External Website
- ◆ Identifiable Subject/Face Within Image
  - ▪ *Image recognition technology*
- ◆ Number of Websites Containing Identical Image
  - ▪ *Beware duplicate content*
- ◆ Embeds of Image on External Website
- ◆ Image Size & Number of Pixels
- ◆ Link Relationship Between Variations or Multiple Versions
  - ▪ *Primary, thumbnails, etc*
- ◆ Number of Times Image Used on Same Website
- ◆ Quality, Aspect Ratio, Entropy, Gradient
- ◆ Total Number of Images on a Page
  - ▪ *More images might be a negative factor*
- ◆ Total Images Linked to from Source Page
- ◆ Total Number of Associated Thumbnails on Source Website

Image ranking factors can become highly technical depending on how determined a campaign manager desires to be. Image optimization strategies can also be easy to implement depending on the resourcefulness and tactical approach employed by the reputation manager.

The following serves as a surgical approach to optimizing an image search vertical with quality, favorable images.

Identifying Image Assets

Approach the image search vertical with similar evaluation and asset organization steps as were described in the "Taking Inventory" stage of the regular search reputation campaign.

Identify positive, neutral, and negative assets within the first 10-20 images results, from left to right and top to bottom priority. Save the source URL of images that are positive and neutral and avoid clicking on obviously negative images. Go ahead and skip the evaluation steps involved in determining image authority or relevance, and focus more on collecting the official source URL of the positive neutral assets in the campaign, as you will use these images in next steps of the strategy.

Creating Image Assets

Similar to the web property asset creation process involved in search reputation strategy, create new images assets that can be used for this component of the campaign.

Source new images from the reputation owner or brand, take photos, create graphics, and collect any offline or protected images that have never been visible or indexed by search engines, as these will serve the campaign well by introducing new quality image content to the search vertical.

Creating image assets offline is only part of the process, as it is necessary to optimize and upload these images to authority properties in order for the search engines to recognize and index them with the campaign.

Publish large, quality, high-resolution versions of these images to the web on authoritative website properties, such as created blogs, press releases, image profile sites like Flickr, and Google+. Publish several uniquely optimized images to each profile, but do not post the same images to the same profiles. Create each profile uniquely with original image content (which also helps these properties in the optimization process for other components of the reputation strategy).

Acquire the source URL of each uploaded image. On a Blogspot or Wordpress blog, images will contain a unique source URL that should be included in a list: (ie: http://mybrandblog.blogspot.com/images/optimized-image-name.jpg). Include these full source URLs of all the high quality, original, uniquely optimized uploaded images from the authority sites they are published to. These URLs will be essential in the promotion process in future steps, so saving these full source URL paths is important.

Ensure the image ranking factor criteria is followed when uploading images to optimized web properties. Using the primary image campaign search phrase, optimize the image file name, the surrounding text or caption, the title, URL, meta data, and text of the page image on which the image is placed. Follow all the optimization criteria of asset creation for regular web properties and embed the image within the content of the page. Display the largest possible pixel dimensions for each image and each page the images are placed on.

Promoting Image Assets

The inventory of images assets collected from image search and through the image creation/upload process should be in the form of the source URLs of the images. This list should contain 10-20 uniquely named (but all optimized) image files hosted on different website properties and pages. Several may be from the same source website but this works best when images are from multiple sources as the search engines will display many images from multiple sources at the top of results, rather than many images from one source.

Engage in content marketing, link building, and social media signal strategies to the pages where the images are hosted, and directly to the images themselves. Include the full source path URL of the images in the linking strategy. Refer to the "Sourcing Links" sections for more information on these tactics.

ProTip: Generate links and social signals directly to the images themselves. This will send undeniable authority metrics to raw image source files that the search engines will have to respond to with higher ranking positions in image search.

In the linking and content marketing strategies, ensure there are combinations of image "embeds" and direct links to the images. Embedding an image in a referring post on another website is properly executed when the image displayed on the other website has a source URL for the image referring back to the target page the image originates from.

The images should always be hosted on the properties controlled by the campaign manager and not re-uploaded to new websites where the image needs to be displayed for content marketing or linking – doing so will conflict with authority signals that need to be sent to the original source. Vary the hyperlinks to the pages hosting the original image and the image itself. Conduct strategic backlink strategies to all pages hosting the original image and embedded images, passing authority directly to and through tiers of republished image content.

"Share" all posted images to social accounts, and Pin every image asset to multiple Pinterest accounts, acquire repins and favorites of images as much as possible (organic or syndicated) and develop as many other social signals as possible to image host pages and directly to images.

There are more tactics involved in infiltrating image search verticals, but the preceding sets of steps are enough to control most image search results for reputation campaigns. Following the steps outlined will also strengthen other aspects of the reputation management strategy, whether a suppression campaign focused on promoting optimized web property assets, or other forms of digital reputation management, as it will allow a brand or person more influence and control over their online "image".

Reputation Campaign Monitoring

Reputation management campaigns involve many moving parts and complex processes that must be executed with precision and control. The interdependent components of the campaign must meet and maintain specific criteria in order for the whole campaign to produce the desired results. Results can vary depending on the nature of search vertical, the campaign objectives, and how the components and processes are executed. Sometimes, variables within the campaign change with and without influence from a campaign manager, so it is important to have methods and tools for monitoring campaign performance objectives.

Monitoring Search Results

Typically, the search results pages for the campaign vertical are the best place to measure and gauge progress and performance. By searching the primary campaign search phrase in the target search engine, results can be viewed and campaign progress measured. This is best done on a weekly or daily basis, depending on how proactive the campaign manager or reputation owner desires to be and how aggressively the strategies of asset creation and promotion are being executed.

If all the steps in the surgical approach provided are being followed, search results pages adjust gradually over the course of several weeks, with positive assets consistently moving upward, and negative listings consistently moving downward. Real-time manual checking of search results pages is most accurate when search engine personalization is turned off, to avoid seeing a different set of 'normal' results based on browser click history and personalization of search results by user account. Search location can be modified as well, which shows different results from different locations in many cases.

Alternative sources of search results page monitoring are available, such as through tools that produce a top 10, or top 20 organic results list for a given search query. There are several accurate "rank checkers" available on the market, the most useful of which are SEMRush.com for small to large organizations, and SearchMetrics.com for larger enterprise organizations.

Monitoring On-Page Changes

Depending on the nature of the campaign property, certain variables can either remain static (unchanging) or may be dynamic (changing). Sometimes critical on-page factors like keyword density, content relevance, and internal and external links can be subject to consistent change based on the way the parent website of the page orchestrates things like related content syndication, releases user-interface changes, or complete redevelopments of website code. These types of code evolutions and dynamic content syndications can sometimes have implications for campaign assets.

Dynamic content features such as related article links, image galleries, social post feeds, and other auto-generated content can influence keyword densities and content relevance, so be sure to monitor campaign assets that have these features and check keyword densities regularly. A shifting keyword density on a campaign asset property represents a risk to the success of the property because an unsuspected increase or decrease in search phrase density could mean the difference of the page ranking in the top 5 results one day, and being demoted to page 2 or lower the next day. Also be sure that dynamic content does not present a liability for the reputation owner in general.

Layout changes are a common byproduct of redevelopments in user-interface design by the parent website hosting a campaign asset page, which can completely change the positive, previously establish optimization factors established by the campaign manager. For example, a website like CrunchBase may completely redevelop their site for a better mobile experience, resulting in changed profile URLs, different positioning of content, different keyword densities, and other critical control variables the campaign manager needs to influence for the property to sustain its value as a campaign asset. Monitor properties for these types of changes to ensure sustainability in ranking factor optimizations on the properties needed for campaign success.

URL changes of target properties are unlikely, but not uncommon changes the campaign manager needs to watch for. A change in the official URL of a campaign property presents several challenges. The hopeful outcome of a URL change is that the parent website properly redirected the former page with a 301 Permanent Redirect protocol, pointing the old page to the new page. This informs the search engines that the old page has been recreated at the new page location, and all attributes of the former page should be attributed to the new page. If done correctly, the inbound link value to the former page will be passed to the new page, however social signal history will not transfer through a 301 redirect, or a canonical URL specification (which is the alternative/acceptable configuration of URL transfer).

If asset properties undergo changes in on-page factors or URL rewrites, be sure to appropriately update assets with on-page changes and linking strategies with new target URLs if the URL changes. Make sure the linking campaign is not still linking to the old property, and begin tracking ranking factors for the new URL.

Monitoring Off-Page Changes

As the linking and inbound social citation strategies evolve, monitor backlink profiles and social signals for every property targeted in the campaign. Using link and social signal analysis tools like Majestic, Moz, Ahrefs, ShareTally, and SharedCount, follow the instructions in the "Link Analysis & Monitoring" and "Monitoring Social Signals" sections to stay ahead of problems and make steady adjustments in sources, authority, anchor text, velocity, recency, and overall quality of inbound signals pointing to each asset property.

Additional Online Reputation Tracking Tools

Feed Reader – Configure a feed reader with custom search phrases that allow the monitoring of content feeds on the iGoogle home page or other feed aggregators.

G Alerts, Y Alerts – Both Google and Yahoo alerts allow tracking of web results, news, blogs, videos, and groups. Configure these tools with custom alert settings to send notifications of relevant content on a topic or search phrase.

Twitter Search – Search Twitter for mentions or comments with any array of search parameters including location, sentiment, dates, links, a particular person, or more.

Technorati – Find mentions of a blog, or specific keywords across other blogs. Subscribe to search results feeds and get notified of mentions.

BackType – Find comments that mention particular words on blogs, and view conversations from particular posts or articles and subscribe to those conversations.

Social Mention – Similar to Google Alerts, social mention is catered towards social media and helps catch immediate conversations and sentiment around a specific keyword.

BoardReader – Allows the tracking of conversations across forums and message boards, with refined results by date, particular domain, and relevance.

Q&A Tracking – Q&A sites like Yahoo Answers allow you to do advanced searches for particular keywords and subscribe to them with RSS feeds at the bottom of the page to keep track of future mentions.

Marketing & Prevention

Once a positive reputation is established, whether recently repaired or genuinely evergreen, a number of mindsets, strategies, and marketing efforts can be employed for sustainability and leverage. As promised and delivered, this book is primarily designed to provide tactical approaches to cleansing and controlling digital reputations in search, however it might be helpful to share a few of the following concepts for maintenance and prevention.

Reputation Marketing

When a company or person has a great reputation, it can be a marketing tool in and of itself. With little to know extra effort, attention placed on a brand or person with a positive reputation has a compounding affect that translates to higher trust, higher engagement, more positive sentiment, increased enthusiasm, and stronger relationship retention.

People want to associate and work with people that are admired by their peers. Consumers want to initiate or continue business relationships with companies that are positively referenced and reviewed by other consumers. Positive reputations are marketing and growth drivers that have immeasurable value for the person or business.

Smart businesses and social-savvy individuals proactively market themselves with their reputation at the forefront. Professional resumes can lead with personal reviews or references of past work and accolades, industry perceptions and past work experience performance highlights, or what they are best known for delivering in terms of quality and results. Business can lead marketing messages with their performance metrics, number of happy customers, what they are best known for, proof of results delivered, history of success, and often lead people to places where these stats can be validated.

Any type of marketing or networking engagement can be artfully crafted with the intent to "sell a reputation" whether engaged by a person or organization. Some say reputation marketing is "the art of selling your great reputation".

Prevention

Most businesses and people facing reputation problems today do not have the luxury of solving their reputation problems with prevention strategies, however it is important to understand several fundamental practices that promote positive experiences with people and consumers that result in better reputation sentiment and prevent more problems from surfacing.

The following will be a series of operational mindsets and core operating values businesses and professionals are encouraged to explore, as many of them can be used to promote a more positive experience with people they engage with in professional or personal affairs.

Ethics

Subject to interpretation, ethics often fortify or corrupt the fundamental operating procedures or conduct of people in business or professional relationships. Taking a journey through the fundamental value system and code of ethics with which an entity operates or conducts business might shed some light on how reputation problems transpire, or could be prevented.

Operations and practices grounded in values like integrity, transparency, compassion, and creative problem solving often lead to higher quality, happier relationships, whereas operational conduct muddied with dishonesty, non-disclosure, defensiveness, and unfairness often result in more problems down the road and are likely the source of current reputation problems that may exist.

Business Model

A business model may effectively serve consumers, other businesses, and active employees. A business model may also negatively impact all people involved, whether internal operatives at a company or anyone the organization transacts business with.

Evaluating a business model and exploring the reciprocal value it provides to people involved, to and from those it conducts business with is a good idea for ensuring its long term sustainability and community sentiment.

There are many books and resources available that provide great insights and models for various types of business models and industries, so it may be worth doing a little bit of extracurricular research and study around what works for a given market or company type.

Customer Service

The way in which a company interfaces with its customers or clients is a large determining factor in how positively or negatively the end user or consumer experiences the brand. Any business who regularly interacts with public consumers around business products or services is strongly encouraged to analyze the entire funnel of customer communications that take place throughout the lifetime of a customer.

Polishing up customer and client communications from staff and automated messaging systems is never a bad idea. Almost always there are ways to provide better information, more clear instructions, provide more resources, answer common questions, and provide more effective guidance and support to people interacting with a business.

Owning Your Negatives

Creative marketers often tackle negative reputations before they start by creating frequently asked questions pages that explain alternatives to the service or product they are offering, or by advance-purchasing domain names that competitors may use to infringe on their brand reputation.

Think creatively about what opportunities are available to spearhead a negative reputation before it starts, and prevent competitors from finding openings in marketing strategy by acquiring any necessary brand assets that could potentially be capitalized on by infringing parties.

Building Credibility

Client testimonials and reviews can be collected, aggregated, and made available on the primary website or business properties to illustrate positive sentiment from other people who have done business with the brand. Collecting and displaying these types of testimonials is a great way to build credibility, along with displaying any industry specific associations or groups that the business participates in. Sometimes a simple logo of a well-known industry group or association extends a certain level of credibility to a new person considering a brand, and can help them overcome resistance in initiating a business relationship.

Responding to Criticism

If negative reviews and comments are taking place, it might be appropriate to respond to them. If someone is generally upset, offer an apology and attempt contact with the person to help resolve his or her issue. Sometimes, a simple and genuine proactive response to a problem is enough to completely resolve a negative complaint, remove it from the Internet, and prevent that person from telling more people about their negative experience.

Accessibility

When people experience problems with a business, their frustration escalates if they cannot contact the organization to resolve the problem and they turn to digital channels of communication to express their frustrations. Providing multiple methods to contact a business is a good idea in the event a customer needs to submit a complaint or seek help. Sometimes, an inquiry is not even a problem until they fail in contacting the organization, resulting in increased frustration and possible reputation problems through digital commenting or posting. Be accessible, respond quickly, or provide clarity on when responses will be provided.

Active Listening

Analytics and monitoring tools provide excellent data on community sentiment and digital conversations taking place about a brand, so use those tools where possible and actively listen to what is being said. Proactive business owners and marketers may also attempt to figure out what the most popular forums and industry groups are related to the business, where the typical customer audience or demographic hangs out, then seeking to participate in conversations on topics and responding to questions, concerns, and providing contributions to the community through those channels.

Centers of Influence

Identify the most industry influencing blogs, forums, and groups relevant to a business or brand and seek to participate in those opportunities. Understandably, a person or business cannot be everywhere at all times, so be selective and determine where the most important conversations are taking place, and take an active role in those communities.

Empowering Others

Many businesses involve friends, family, co-workers, and business partners in online reputation management efforts. There are many people in the close warm circle of an organization that can make great contributions with positive sentiment to an entity's online reputation. Determine who these people might be, identify the areas they can influence, and empower them to contribute.

Philanthropy

Social responsibility is often limited to a communication and public service mindset, but in reality an organization can make any number of philanthropic contributions to the public, non-profits, charities, and organizations that are important to the community being served.

Identifying areas to make philanthropic contributions and taking advantage of these opportunities is a great way to inspire positive sentiment around an organization or company. With philanthropic activities, a business can create more opportunities for reputation marketing.

Congruency of Values & Action

After a thorough evaluation of core values and operating procedures that govern a company's actions, follow through and validate that the actions being taken are congruent with those values. There is nothing that will kill a positive reputation faster than actions and conduct that do not match the ethics and operational values that a company promises to deliver.

Add Value

Whether online or offline, a business or organization should be clear on what value it provides to the public, to consumers, to other businesses, to its employees, and what value it gains in return. Creating value is important for maintaining a positive reputation in any business operation; otherwise the business might not succeed. Identify the areas of value contribution that a company is best at, and strengthen those contributions where possible. If no value is being added, then a business model evaluation might be in order.

Serve An Audience

Creating great content and building a community of followers do not have to be divided business processes, and both produce more benefits when intertwined and proactively combined. Encourage fans to engage newly content, and use content to engage a new audience. Share new content with fans on social media, and strategically develop content that will gain the attention of a new slice of the industry. Doing so will propel the growth of followers and will help retain an existing audience.

Reciprocate Positivity

People like to feel appreciated and encouraged when they do or say something positive, so respond to people's positive reviews and comments by reciprocating appreciation for them in return. A simple "thank you, we appreciate your business!" goes a long way with people because it let's them know their comment was received and appreciated. Take advantage of opportunities to reciprocate positive support and make it public. Other viewers of the communication exchange will experience the positive exchange, which will encourage them to sustain or initiate a relationship.

Helpful Humility

Always be helping, and always be humble. Help those that can be helped or need help, and maintain an attitude of humility in public communications. Let the demonstration of action and helpfulness do the talking, and avoid boasting about greatness and status. People will perceive excellence through the demonstration of action, not claims. Utilize an operating mindset of helpfulness to over-deliver on expectations and exceed the status quo. Show people what greatness looks like, and define it through action.

Keep Good Company

The behavior of friends, employees, associates, business partners, and sponsors can have a way of creeping into a business' reputation online. Be mindful and aware of the actions taken by those in association with a brand and stay alert to changes that may impact the trajectory of the entity's digital reputation. Take inventory of communication channels and identify areas of weakness or opportunity. Monitor and correct where appropriate.

Identify Weaknesses

Determine any sources of reputation liability and seek to eradicate potential reputation problems before they happen. Weaknesses may be uncovered through customer or employee surveys, by analyzing competitor reputations and the problems they have faced, and by evaluating the history of the organization and the problems it has experienced since inception. Find ways to strengthen or compensate for areas of weakness and try to avoid letting these liabilities turn into reputation problems.

Be Better

A business or person that does not learn from past mistakes or reputation problems will continue to experience more of the same inconveniences in the future. Always attempt to make corrective action around the originating source of the problem rather than constantly playing the defense. The nature of a reputation problem only repeats itself if the person or business repeats the same behavior that caused the problem in the first place. Tease out solutions to problems and engage in appropriate education and training for the areas that need to be improved. Consistently doing so will result in perpetual growth and betterment in people and the company.

Thank you

Thank you for your interest in reputation management and search engine optimization. Thank you for taking a proactive approach to your role and reputation in our digital world. I know that the information contained in this book can be overwhelmingly complex and technical, but I have full confidence in your ability to use it to improve your life and business.

Now that you have read this book, and have access to some of the most advanced tactics for digital reputation management, you have every opportunity to catapult towards success.

Take it one step at a time. Do the most important things first. Set goals for yourself and try not to get overwhelmed with the minutia. Follow the process outlined in the surgical approach, and feel free to reach out if you need help.

I love helping people with SEO and reputation management. There is nothing that makes me experience more joy than empowering people to use what I have so passionately dedicated myself to for over 15 years. And please, if you find yourself resisting the amount of work involved, are fearful of not getting results, or for any reason would prefer to have my team provide you the help you need...

Just ask.

Consider the coaching group as a powerful resource, and learn more about our done for you services if you need help.

Thanks again,
Tyler Collins

Reputation Black Box

An Unusual Invitation...

Dear Marketer,

This is an invitation.. But it's not an ordinary invitation. When ordinary invitations are sent out, it's the desire of the host that all who receive his invitation accept it and are able to attend. This one is different.

Hi, my name is Tyler Collins... It's nice to meet you. My "day job" is CEO of SwellMarketing.com, but I also serve as Chairman of the most elite online reputation coaching group.

It's called: **Reputation Black Box**

Veteran digital marketers, wicked smart branding experts, C-Level SEO consultants, media moguls and publishers, traffic & conversion experts, affiliate marketers, funnel experts, and seasoned CEO's are just a sample of who's involved in this super secret, training intensive, cutting-edge strategy coaching program.

Reputation Black Box is not for everyone, and frankly, not everyone who applies is accepted. But if you do manage to get in, you'll have access to the most powerful reputation tactics in the industry, dozens of campaign automation tools, in-depth implementation training, and me.

You will not find anyone else who has spent over 10 years mastering online reputation management, spent millions of dollars testing and PROVING strategies that work in hundreds of industries for thousands of clients, who's willing to give you this type of training, hand-holding, resource sharing, strategy exposing, and exclusive attention.

I guarantee it.

Every month, by phone and email, you and I will take an intimate look at your campaigns together. You'll have my undivided attention to help you formulate customized strategies for successfully removing negative content from search for any campaign, in any industry, and at great speed.

Reputation Black Box gives you access to:

- The exact training I give my own team to save you years of frustration and headaches.
- The secret automation tools we use to cut days & weeks of work down to hours.
- Proven turnkey campaign templates so you can quickly and efficiently rollout tactics.
- Reporting tools and templates so you can monitor and report to clients effectively.
- Exclusive access to me for YOUR CAMPAIGNS for 1hr per month, with email support.
- Access to MY TEAM for follow up training/consulting/guidance.
- The newest, effective, strategies and tools we use so don't have to worry about having to adapt and change. We stay ahead of the game, so you don't have to.
- Additional digital marketing consulting and resources - If I have it, you get it.

Here's the caveat...

I'm going to hold you accountable. I insist on your success if you're in my group, so I'm going to make sure you do everything you need to, in the right way, at the right time, with the right help in order to be successful.

Also, this group is limited to 50 people. Coaching 50 people on 50 or more different reputation campaigns requires thought, time, diligence, attention, and careful planning, so I have to make sure the group is neatly contained in an elite group of 50.

50 People. That's it.

I love this part of my business. Helping people succeed is in my DNA and I hope you become one of the people I help and transform.

For more information and application to become one of my students, visit:

ORMBook.com/BlackBox

Sincerely,

Tyler Collins
Chairman, Reputation Black Box

P.S. Have you heard the expression "Knowledge is Power?"

I disagree. Knowledge is only as powerful as your means and ability to execute on it. Apply to my coaching program and let me show you how to be unstoppable online.

Done For You Services

There are many "reputation management companies" who provide services to people and businesses in need of reputation repair. Proceed with caution as very few of them use many, if any, of the proven tactical solutions explained in this book.

If you are seeking a reliable team with years of experience in digital marketing, search engine optimization, and reputation management, please reach out to our team at **Swell Marketing, Inc (swellmarketing.com)** for a free consultation on your reputation opportunity.

Swell Marketing handles some of the toughest SEO and reputation management campaigns in the nation. From Fortune 500 companies to small businesses and high profile executives, our firm provides effective SEO results for businesses looking to increase qualified traffic or cleanup negative content from search.

We have proven our results in over 140 different industries, and help thousands of businesses per year. With a 100% success rate with over 1,000 clients we have an unfair advantage to help any business or person that needs results in search.

We provide reputation services for lawyers, doctors, movie stars, and musicians, even politicians. The results we are asked to repair, some would say are impossible, but we do it everyday.

The major difference between our reputation management services and some of the other companies out there is that we actually have a realistic assessment of what it takes to influence top search results. Most companies don't have a clue, or just do the bare minimum, which is seldom enough to create the desired result. Our teams of 37 experts have been active practitioners for over 15 years.

We relentlessly study search technology, evolve with the changes, and sustain results - we go as far as studying Google patents on organic search on weekly basis.

Visit **SwellMarketing.com** for a free consultation.

About The Author

Tyler Collins is a digital marketer by trade, SEO consultant at heart, online reputation expert by demand, and pilots several successful tech ventures. Highly sought after by Fortune 500 companies, C-level executives, and online marketing "gurus" seeking the most cutting-edge tactics for search engine placement and online reputation management.

Over 15 years of Internet marketing & search engine optimization, Tyler has built dozens of successful digital media teams, and delivers results for over 3,000 clients in over 130 different industries.

Founder of Swell Marketing Inc, a full-spectrum digital agency fulfilling online marketing and Internet application development services to thousands of companies, providing turn-key white-label services and training for SEO companies and delivering silent back-end SEO processes for dozens of front facing SEO firms.

National speaker, author, and online marketing mentor, Tyler specializes in analyzing, planning & executing ROI driven marketing programs for small, medium, and large websites. Clients include companies like NIKE, Hurley, Charles Schwabb, CocaCola, Dermalogica, Tracfone, O'Neill, Abraham Group, and dozens of Fortune 500 companies.

Board Director at Surfline.com, a global surf media website powered by marine weather and wave forecasting technology, providing international reporting with hundreds of live, high definition streaming cams around the globe.

Outside the professional sector, Tyler is a life coach and mentor to young adults, and gives regular motivational talks at high schools. He is an avid surfer, scuba diver, and environmentalist. He is considered a "process nut", always seeking to define the right formula for everything in life, and often sees the sunrise while reading Google's latest organic search algorithm patent, washed down with some strong black coffee.

Professional Website:	www.tyler-collins.com
Connect On LinkedIn:	www.linkedin.com/in/tylermcollins
Reputation Resources:	www.ormbook.com
Done For You Services:	www.swellmarketing.com

Legal Notice

We are not affiliated with Google, Bing, Yahoo, or other companies that may be featured within this document.

All trademarks belong to their respective owners.

No earnings claims are being made anywhere in this report or in the marketing of this report.

The publisher and author is not liable for any damages or losses associated with the content of this report, the outcomes of any strategies explained, or any supporting media featured, produced, or focused from this report.

Limits of Liability & Disclaimer

Understand that this document and any accompanying media are not attempting to dispense professional and/or legal advice. Please note that it is your responsibility to determine if the strategies contained within this book/report are right for you and your business.

References

"Rich Snippets" ;)

Search Patent Grants & Applications

US Patent 7,584,177
Title: "Determination of a desired repository" September 1, 2009
Inventors: Angelo; Michael (San Francisco, CA), Braginsky; David (Mountain View, CA), Ginsberg; Jeremy (San Francisco, CA), Tong; Simon (Mountain View, CA)
Assignee: Google Inc. (Mountain View, CA)
Source: http://patft.uspto.gov/netacgi/nph-Parser?Sect1=PTO2&Sect2=HITOFF&p=1&u=%2Fnetahtml%2FPTO%2Fsearch-adv.htm&r=1&f=G&l=50&d=PALL&S1=07584177&OS=PN/07584177&RS=PN/07584177

US Patent 7,302,645
Title: "Methods and systems for identifying manipulated articles," November 27, 2007
Inventors: Henzinger; Monika (Corseaux, CH), Franz; Alexander Mark (Palo Alto, CA)
Assignee: Google Inc. (Mountain View, CA)
Source: http://patft.uspto.gov/netacgi/nph-Parser?Sect1=PTO2&Sect2=HITOFF&p=1&u=%2Fnetahtml%2FPTO%2Fsearch-adv.htm&r=1&f=G&l=50&d=PALL&S1=07302645&OS=PN/07302645&RS=PN/07302645

US Patent 8,244,722
Title: "Ranking documents" August 14, 2012
Inventors: Koningstein; Ross (Menlo Park, CA)
Assignee: Google Inc. (Mountain View, CA)
Source: http://patft.uspto.gov/netacgi/nph-Parser?Sect1=PTO2&Sect2=HITOFF&p=1&u=%2Fnetahtml%2FPTO%2Fsearch-adv.htm&r=1&f=G&l=50&d=PALL&S1=08244722&OS=PN/08244722&RS=PN/08244722

US Patent 9,165,040
Title: "Producing a ranking for pages using distances in a web-link graph" October 20, 2015
Applicant: Hajaj; Nissan
Assignee: Google Inc. (Mountain View, CA)
Source: http://patft.uspto.gov/netacgi/nph-Parser?Sect1=PTO1&Sect2=HITOFF&d=PALL&p=1&u=%2Fnetahtml%2FPTO2Fsrchnum.htm&r=1&f=G&l=50&s1=9,165,040.PN.&OS=PN/9,165,040&RS=PN/9,165,040

US Patent Application 60/035,205
Title: "Improved Text Searching in Hypertext Systems"
Inventor: Page; Lawrence
Source: http://www.seobythesea.com/improved-text-searching-in-hypertext-systems.pdf
Concept: Original Page Rank Patent

US Patent 6,285,999
Title: "Method for node ranking in a linked database" September 4, 2001
Inventors: Page; Lawrence (Stanford, CA)
Assignee: The Board of Trustees of the Leland Stanford Junior University (Stanford, CA)
Source: http://patft.uspto.gov/netacgi/nph-Parser?Sect1=PTO2&Sect2=HITOFF&u=%2Fnetahtml%2FPTO%2Fsearch-adv.htm&r=1&p=1&f=G&l=50&d=PTXT&S1=6,285,999.PN.&OS=pn/6,285,999&RS=PN/6,285,999

US Patent 7,058,628
Title: "Method for node ranking in a linked database" June 6, 2006
Inventors: Page; Lawrence (Stanford, CA)
Assignee: The Board of Trustees of the Leland Stanford Junior University (Palo Alto, CA)
Source: http://patft.uspto.gov/netacgi/nph-Parser?Sect1=PTO2&Sect2=HITOFF&u=%2Fnetahtml%2FPTO%2Fsearch-adv.htm&r=1&p=1&f=G&l=50&d=PTXT&S1=7,058,628.PN.&OS=pn/7,058,628&RS=PN/7,058,628

US Patent 6,799,176
Title: "Method for scoring documents in a linked database" September 28, 2004
Inventors: Page; Lawrence (Stanford, CA)
Assignee: The Board of Trustees of the Leland Stanford Junior University (Palo Alto, CA)
Source: http://patft.uspto.gov/netacgi/nph-Parser?Sect1=PTO2&Sect2=HITOFF&u=%2Fnetahtml%2FPTO%2Fsearch-adv.htm&r=1&p=1&f=G&l=50&d=PTXT&S1=6,799,176.PN.&OS=pn/6,799,176&RS=PN/6,799,176

US Patent 7,269,587
Title: "Scoring documents in a linked database" September 11, 2007
Inventors: Page; Lawrence (Stanford, CA)
Assignee: The Board of Trustees of the Leland Stanford Junior University (Palo Alto, CA)
Source: http://patft.uspto.gov/netacgi/nph-Parser?Sect1=PTO2&Sect2=HITOFF&u=%2Fnetahtml%2FPTO%2Fsearch-adv.htm&r=1&p=1&f=G&l=50&d=PTXT&S1=7,269,587.PN.&OS=pn/7,269,587&RS=PN/7,269,587

US Patent 7,269,587
Title: "Annotating links in a document based on the ranks of documents pointed to by the links" March 15, 2011
Inventors: Page; Lawrence (Stanford, CA)
Assignee: The Board of Trustees of the Leland Stanford Junior University (Palo Alto, CA)
Source: http://patft.uspto.gov/netacgi/nph-Parser?Sect1=PTO2&Sect2=HITOFF&u=%2Fnetahtml%2FPTO%2Fsearch-adv.htm&r=1&p=1&f=G&l=50&d=PTXT&S1=7,908,277.PN.&OS=pn/7,908,277&RS=PN/7,908,277

US Patent 9,165,030
Title: "Showing prominent users for information retrieval requests" October 20, 2015
Inventors: Hung; Wanda Wen-hui (Los Gatos, CA), Gong; Jun (San Jose, CA), Dorohonceanu; Bogdan (Somerset, NJ), Kamdar; Sagar (Redwood City, CA), Hansson; Othar (Sunnyvale, CA)
Assignee: Google Inc. (Mountain View, CA)
Source: http://patft.uspto.gov/netacgi/nph-Parser?Sect1=PTO1&Sect2=HITOFF&d=PALL&p=1&u=%2Fnetahtml%2FPTO%2Fsrchnum.htm&r=1&l=G&l=50&s1=9,165,030.PN.&OS=PN/9,165,030&RS=PN/9,165,030
Concept: Authoritative Rank

US Patent 7,565,358
Title: "Agent Rank" July 21, 2009
Inventors: Minogue; David (Palo Alto, CA), Tucker; Paul A. (Mountain View, CA)
Assignee: Google Inc. (Mountain View, CA)
Source: http://patft.uspto.gov/netacgi/nph-Parser?Sect1=PTO2&Sect2=HITOFF&p=1&u=%2Fnetahtml%2FPTO%2Fsearch-adv.htm&r=1&f=G&l=50&d=PALL&S1=07565358&OS=PN/07565358&RS=PN/07565358
Concept: Author Rank

US Patent 8,719,276
Title: "Ranking nodes in a linked database based on node independence" May 6, 2014
Inventors: Haahr; Paul (San Francisco, CA), Kaszkiel; Martin (Santa Clara, CA), Singhal; Amit (Palo Alto, CA)
Assignee: Google Inc. (Mountain View, CA)
Source: http://patft.uspto.gov/netacgi/nph-Parser?Sect1=PTO2&Sect2=HITOFF&p=1&u=%2Fnetahtml%2FPTO%2Fsearch-adv.htm&r=1&f=G&l=50&d=PALL&S1=08719276&OS=PN/08719276&RS=PN/08719276
Concept: Google Paid Link Patent

US Patent 7,783,639
Title: "Determining quality of linked documents" August 24, 2010
Inventors: Bharat; Krishna (San Jose, CA), Singhal; Amit (Palo Alto, CA), Haahr; Paul (San Francisco, CA)
Assignee: Google Inc. (Mountain View, CA)
Source: http://patft.uspto.gov/netacgi/nph-Parser?Sect1=PTO2&Sect2=HITOFF&u=%2Fnetahtml%2FPTO%2Fsearch-adv.htm&r=1&p=1&f=G&l=50&d=PTXT&S1=7,783,639.PN.&OS=pn/7,783,639&RS=PN/7,783,639
Concept: Affiliate Link Patent

US Patent Application 20080010281
Title: "User-sensitive pagerank" January 10, 2008
Inventors: Berkhin; Pavel; (Sunnyvale, CA) ; Fayyad; Usama M.; (Sunnyvale, CA) ; Raghavan; Prabhakar; (Saratoga, CA) ; Tomkins; Andrew; (San Jose, CA)
Assignee: YAHOO! INC.
Source: http://appft1.uspto.gov/netacgi/nph-Parser?Sect1=PTO2&Sect2=HITOFF&u=%2Fnetahtml%2FPTO%2Fsearch-adv.html&r=1&p=1&f=G&l=50&d=PG01&S1=20080010281.PGNR.&OS=dn/20080010281&RS=DN/20080010281

US Patent 7,536,382
Title: "Query rewriting with entity detection" May 19, 2009
Inventors: Zhou; Hong (Sunnyvale, CA), Bharat; Krishna (San Jose, CA), Schmitt; Michael (Newfalm, DE), Curtiss; Michael (Sunnyvale, CA), Mayer; Marissa (Palo Alto, CA)
Assignee: Google Inc. (Mountain View, CA)
Source: http://patft.uspto.gov/netacgi/nph-Parser?Sect1=PTO2&Sect2=HITOFF&u=%2Fnetahtml%2FPTO%2Fsearch-adv.htm&r=1&p=1&f=G&l=50&d=PTXT&S1=7,536,382.PN.&OS=pn/7,536,382&RS=PN/7,536,382

US Patent 7,895,148
Title: "Classifying functions of web blocks based on linguistic features" February 22, 2011
Inventors: Ma; Wei-Ying (Beijing, CN), Xiao; Xiangye (Beijing, CN), Xie; Xing (Beijing, CN)
Assignee: Microsoft Corporation (Redmond, WA)
Source: http://patft.uspto.gov/netacgi/nph-Parser?Sect1=PTO2&Sect2=HITOFF&u=%2Fnetahtml%2FPTO%2Fsearch-adv.htm&r=1&p=1&f=G&l=50&d=PTXT&S1=7,895,148.PN.&OS=PN/7,895,148&RS=PN/7,895,148

US Patent 7,350,187
Title: "System and methods for automatically creating lists " March 25, 2008
Inventors: Tong; Simon (Mountain View, CA), Dean; Jeff (Menlo Park, CA)
Assignee: Google Inc. (Mountain View, CA)
Source: http://patft.uspto.gov/netacgi/nph-Parser?Sect1=PTO2&Sect2=HITOFF&u=%2Fnetahtml%2FPTO%2Fsearch-adv.htm&r=1&p=1&f=G&l=50&d=PTXT&S1=7,350,187.PN.&OS=pn/7,350,187&RS=PN/7,350,187

US Patent 7,913,163
Title: "Determining semantically distinct regions of a document" March 22, 2011
Inventors: Zunger; Yonatan (Mountain View, CA)
Assignee: Google Inc. (Mountain View, CA)
Source: http://patft.uspto.gov/netacgi/nph-Parser?Sect1=PTO2&Sect2=HITOFF&p=1&u=%2Fnetahtml%2FPTO%2Fsearch-adv.htm&r=1&f=G&l=50&d=PALL&S1=07913163&OS=PN/07913163&RS=PN/07913163

US Patent 8,086,600
Title: "Interleaving search results" December 27, 2011
Inventors: Bailey; David R. (Palo Alto, CA), Effrat; Jonathan J. (Mountain View, CA), Singhal; Amit (Palo Alto, CA)
Assignee: Google Inc. (Mountain View, CA)
Source: http://patft.uspto.gov/netacgi/nph-Parser?Sect1=PTO2&Sect2=HITOFF&p=1&u=%2Fnetahtml%2FPTO%2Fsearch-adv.htm&r=1&f=G&l=50&d=PALL&S1=08086600&OS=PN/08086600&RS=PN/08086600

US Patent 8,055,669
Title: "Search queries improved based on query semantic information" November 8, 2011
Inventors: Singhal; Amit (Palo Alto, CA), Sahami; Mehran (Redwood City, CA), Lamping; John (Los Altos, CA), Kaszkiel; Marcin (Santa Clara, CA), Henzinger; Monika H. (Menlo Park, CA)
Assignee: Google Inc. (Mountain View, CA)
Source: http://patft.uspto.gov/netacgi/nph-Parser?Sect1=PTO2&Sect2=HITOFF&p=1&u=%2Fnetahtml%2FPTO%2Fsearch-adv.htm&r=1&f=G&l=50&d=PALL&S1=08055669&OS=PN/08055669&RS=PN/08055669

US Patent 7,636,714
Title: "Determining query term synonyms within query context" December 22, 2009
Inventors: Lamping; John (Los Altos, CA), Baker; Steven (San Francisco, CA)
Assignee: Google Inc. (Mountain View, CA)
Source: http://patft.uspto.gov/netacgi/nph-Parser?Sect1=PTO2&Sect2=HITOFF&p=1&u=%2Fnetahtml%2FPTO%2Fsearch-adv.htm&r=1&f=G&l=50&d=PALL&S1=07636714&OS=PN/07636714&RS=PN/07636714

US Patent Application 20080319962
Title: "Machine Translation for Query Expansion" December 25, 2008
Inventors: Riezler; Stefan; (Menlo Park, CA) ; Vasserman; Alexander L.; (Malden, MA)
Assignee: GOOGLE INC.
Source: http://appft.uspto.gov/netacgi/nph-Parser?Sect1=PTO2&Sect2=HITOFF&u=%2Fnetahtml%2FPTO%2Fsearch-adv.html&r=1&p=1&f=G&l=50&d=PG01&S1=20080319962.PGNR.&OS=dn/20080319962&RS=DN/20080319962

US Patent 9104750 B1
Title: "Using concepts as contexts for query term substitutions" Aug 11, 2015
Inventors: Kedar Dhamdhere, Thomas Strohmann, P. Pandurang Nayak, Robert Spalek
Assignee: Google Inc.
Source: https://www.google.com/patents/US9104750
Concept: RankBrain

US Patent 9,189,526
Title: "Freshness based ranking" November 17, 2015
Inventors: Chen; Zhihui (Menlo Park, CA), Frankle; Jonathan (Los Gatos, CA)
Assignee: Google Inc. (Mountain View, CA)
Source: http://patft.uspto.gov/netacgi/nph-Parser?Sect1=PTO1&Sect2=HITOFF&d=PALL&p=1&u=%2Fnetahtml%2FPTO%2Fsrchnum.htm&r=1&f=G&l=50&s1=9,189,526.PN.&OS=PN/9,189,526&RS=PN/9,189,526

US Patent 8,682,892
Title: "Ranking search results" March 25, 2014
Inventors: Panda; Navneet (Mountain View, CA), Ofitserov; Vladimir (Foster City, CA)
Assignee: Google Inc. (Mountain View, CA)
Source: http://patft.uspto.gov/netacgi/nph-Parser?Sect1=PTO2&Sect2=HITOFF&p=1&u=%2Fnetahtml%2FPTO%2Fsearch-adv.htm&r=1&f=G&l=50&d=PALL&S1=08682892&OS=PN/08682892&RS=PN/08682892

Internet Publications, Academic Papers & Books

Google, Inc. (2007) "Google Begins to Move to Universal Search", MOUNTAIN VIEW, Calif.
URL: http://googlepress.blogspot.com/2007/05/google-begins-move-to-universal-search_16.html

Marissa Mayer. (2007) "Universal search: The best answer is still the best answer", Google Official Blog
URL: https://googleblog.blogspot.com/2007/05/universal-search-best-answer-is-still.html

David Bailey. (2007) "Behind the scenes with universal search," Google Official Blog
URL: https://googleblog.blogspot.com/2007/05/behind-scenes-with-universal-search.html

Marcus Tober, Daniel Furch, Kai Londenberg, Luca Massaron, Jan Grundmann. (2015)
"Search Ranking Factors and Rank Correlations, Google U.S. 2015" - SearchMetrics
URL: http://www.searchmetrics.com/knowledge-base/ranking-factors/

Marcus Tober, Daniel Furch. (2015) "Universal Search, Google Products on the Rise" - SearchMetrics
URL: http://www.searchmetrics.com/knowledge-base/universal-search-study/

Matt Cutts. (2012) "Another step to reward high-quality sites", Google Webmaster Central Blog
URL: http://googlewebmastercentral.blogspot.com/2012/04/another-step-to-reward-high-quality.html

Brin; Sergey, Page; Lawrence. "The anatomy of a large-scale hypertextual web search engine."
World-Wide Web Conference, Bris-bane, Australia, April 1998.

Pinkerton; Brian. "Finding what people want: Experiences with the web crawler."
World-Wide Web Conference, Chicago, Illinois, October 1994

Becchetti; Luca, Castillo; Carlos, Donato; Debora, Baeza-Yates; Ricardo, "Link-Based Characterization and Detection of Web Spam" August 10, 2006
URL: http://airweb.cse.lehigh.edu/2006/becchetti.pdf
Concept: Truncated PageRank Concept

Haveliwala; Taher H. "Topic Sensitive PageRank", (2002) Stanford University
URL: http://ilpubs.stanford.edu:8090/573/1/2002-6.pdf
Concept: PageRank Calculations by Topic Relevance

Langville; Amy N., Meyer; Carl D., "Google's PageRank and Beyond: The Science of Search Engine Rankings" (2012)
URL: http://press.princeton.edu/titles/8216.html
Concept: PageRank and Ranking Positions

Kamvar; Sepandar D., Haveliwala; Taher H., Manning; Christopher D., Golub; Gene H., "Exploiting the Block Structure of the Web for Computing PageRank " (2003)
URL: http://nlp.stanford.edu/pubs/blockrank.pdf
Concept: BlockRank

Jing ; Yushi, Baluja; Shumeet, "PageRank for Product Image Search" (2008) Beijing, China
URL: http://www.www2008.org/papers/pdf/p307-jingA.pdf

Junghoo; Cho Hector, Garcia-Molina, Page; Lawrence, "Efficient CrawlingThrough URL Ordering" (2001)
URL: http://oak.cs.ucla.edu/~cho/papers/cho-order.pdf

Gy-ongyi; Zoltan, Garcia-Molina; Hector, Pedersen; Jan. "Combating Web Spam with TrustRank" (2004)
URL: http://www.vldb.org/conf/2004/RS15P3.PDF

Berhkin; Pavel, "A Survey on PageRank Computing" Internet Mathematics Vol. 2, No. 1: 73-120 (2005)
URL: http://www.cs.kent.edu/~javed/class-CXNET09S/papers-CXNET-2009/Berk05-Berkhin.pdf

"Online Reputation in a Connected World," Microsoft; Cross-Tab, 2010
URL: http://download.microsoft.com/download/E/0/9/E094917B-049C-4B00-AE65-E97F55585C08/DPD_Online%20Reputation%20Research_overview.doc.

Slawski; Bill. Patent Research, Articles, & Resources
URL: http://www.seobythesea.com/

"Google Algorithm Change History" 2000-2015, SEOmoz, Inc
URL: https://moz.com/google-algorithm-change

Index

Criteria, 21, 52, 76, 83, 89, 95-97, 101, 103, 108-109, 115, 128, 138, 143, 146, 150, 159-161, 169, 171-173, 180, 202, 204-205, 216, 222-223, 226, 229
Criticism, 236
Crowd, 222
Crunchbase, 149, 160, 162, 230
Crusade, 11, 27
CTR (click through rate), 90-91, 174
Custom, 152-154, 159, 215, 232
Customer, 7, 12-13, 21, 25, 54, 59, 72, 99, 128, 176, 186-187, 214, 233, 235, 237, 240
Customization, 141, 152
Cutts, 250
Cxnet, 250
Cyber, 38

D

Dailymotion, 153
Damage, 20, 33, 41, 51-52, 58, 94, 124, 128, 163, 200, 202, 204, 245
Damage campaign properties, 204
Danger, 29
Data, 1, 8, 48, 74, 82, 85, 88, 90, 93, 108, 113-115, 117, 146, 186, 207-208, 213, 224, 226, 237
Database, 11, 36, 155, 246-247
Date, 18, 81, 150, 154, 157, 159, 232
Debate, 31, 117
Debunking, 187
Decade, 5, 59
Deceive, 33
Decide, 12, 18, 93, 137, 141, 176, 206, 208
Decisions, 1, 9, 12-14, 16, 19, 27, 32, 58, 66, 93, 134, 156
Decline, 118
Deconstruct, 106
Decrease, 21, 104, 118, 211, 230
Dedicated, 7, 38, 42, 46, 49, 62, 98, 103, 155, 223, 244
Deep, 4, 64, 107, 109, 123
Defame, 40
Default, 9, 40, 46, 172
Defeat, 111
Defend, 34
Deficiencies, 105, 133
Define, 124, 127, 135-136, 139, 142, 191, 240
Delays, 89
Deleted, 23, 117
Delineations, 56
Deliver, 22, 43, 71, 93, 112, 167, 238, 240
Demand, 11-12, 18, 23, 66, 75, 90, 113, 117, 122, 129, 222
Demographic, 237
Demonstration, 240
Demotion, 109, 200
Denial, 24
Depending, 16, 23, 31, 47, 49-50, 57, 59-60, 72, 81, 85, 88, 105, 107, 116, 124, 141, 145-147, 149, 151-153, 193, 195, 202, 225, 229-230

Deploy, 78, 220
Deprecated, 189
Depth, 22, 86, 163
Derived, 64, 97, 103, 107, 115, 130, 189, 209, 213
Descending, 211
Described, 74, 130, 136-137, 140, 142, 155-156, 167, 169, 180, 189, 194, 205, 208-210, 224-225
Description, 88, 140-142, 146-148, 150, 152, 154-156, 159, 206, 215, 217, 220
Description Hyperlinks, 154
Deserve, 70-71, 73, 98, 108, 163, 165, 194
Design, 39, 82, 144, 152, 230
Designated, 38, 177-178, 199
Designed, 4, 19, 22, 24-25, 44, 49, 60, 68, 74, 99, 105, 109, 163, 166, 206, 214, 220, 233
Destination, 108
Destroy, 4
Detect, 24, 73, 100, 105, 172, 204
Detection, 204, 248, 250
Determine, 52, 54-56, 64, 83-84, 86-87, 93, 95, 100, 107, 119, 125, 138-139, 144, 158, 161, 169, 172, 206, 210, 215, 237-238, 240, 245
Determined, 17, 31, 71, 81, 94, 97-98, 107, 130, 162, 189, 225
Determining, 57, 67, 107-108, 132-133, 170, 172-174, 176, 180, 189, 225, 235, 248-249
Detrimental, 12, 26, 54, 128
Devaluation, 161
Developed, 36, 81, 107, 142, 188-189, 195, 206
Development, 7, 17, 30, 82, 176, 193
Device, 9, 23, 54
Different, 3, 5, 33, 36-37, 42, 48-49, 52, 55-57, 59, 63, 68, 70-71, 85-87, 95-96, 102-103, 105-107, 109, 116, 124-125, 129, 141-143, 146, 166, 170, 174, 188, 191, 193, 204-205, 207, 209, 211, 214, 218, 224, 227, 229-230, 243
Difficult, 4, 32, 46, 48, 63, 72, 76, 93, 130, 133, 188, 203, 205
Digital, 2, 4-5, 7-8, 10-11, 13-17, 20, 23, 25, 30, 33, 36-37, 42, 48, 50, 54, 57, 61, 63, 65-66, 70, 113, 123, 128, 160, 163-165, 176-177, 184, 214, 228, 233, 237, 240, 243-244
Digitally, 184
Dilution, 212
Dimensions, 226
Directory, 95, 120, 165, 179, 193-194, 204, 220
Disable, 154
Disadvantages, 14
Disappearance, 104, 209
Disaster, 187
Disavow, 104-105
Disbarred, 36
Disclaimer, 42, 58, 245
Discontinuations, 189
Discussion, 31, 44, 154, 159
Disgruntled, 49
Dishonest, 25
Dishonesty, 234

262

266

R

Race, 38
Radio, 185
Random, 97, 106, 173
Range, 18, 43, 45, 75, 94, 98, 109, 139, 207, 210
Rank, 1, 6, 69, 73, 80, 82, 91, 94, 96, 113, 148, 163-164, 168, 170-172, 174, 188, 195, 223-224, 230, 246-247, 250
Rankbrain, 249
Ranked, 59, 138, 171-172
Ranking, 22, 59, 63, 71-74, 76, 78-83, 85-87, 89-90, 92-99, 101, 104-106, 108-110, 113-115, 117-119, 122-123, 133, 136, 139-140, 142, 146, 150-153, 160-161, 163-164, 166-168, 170-172, 174-175, 188-189, 191, 199-200, 202-207, 210-219, 221-227, 230-231, 246-247,
Ranking factors, 22, 72, 78, 80, 82, 90, 92, 94, 140, 205, 223
Ranking positions, 73, 85, 90, 98-99, 109, 117, 163-64, 166, 172, 174, 191, 210-12, 250
Ranking target properties, 214
Rate, 30, 90-91, 174, 186, 194, 202, 209
Ratings, 21, 50, 122
Ratio, 224
Readable, 45, 49
Reader, 7, 19, 27, 43, 65, 84, 182, 232
Readership, 35
Reality, 5, 12, 28-29, 40, 161-162, 201, 238
Reason, 4, 8, 10, 31, 39-42, 97, 103, 105, 107, 111-112, 125, 139, 171-172, 211, 244
Rebranding, 19, 186
Rebuilt, 158
Recency, 71, 105, 113, 116-117, 150, 213, 221, 231
Recent, 29, 71-72, 88, 103-104, 119, 152, 154, 159, 187, 191, 220
Reciprocal, 235
Recognition, 73, 86, 94-95, 121, 144, 219, 221-222, 224
Recommendation, 52, 54, 138, 140-141, 148, 150, 175, 179, 191, 206, 216
Recommended, 4, 13, 53, 83, 147-148, 152, 157, 160, 176, 194, 204-207, 212, 216
Record, 11, 36, 39, 46, 63, 65, 71, 74
Recover, 205
Recreate, 4
Redirect, 231
Redistributed, 85
Redundancies, 141
Refer, 66, 68, 83-84, 105, 124-125, 129, 133, 139-140, 142, 146, 149, 163, 169-170, 210, 219, 227
Reference, 6, 16, 46, 54-55, 80, 94-95, 113, 120, 183, 220, 224, 233, 246
Referral, 186
Referring, 96, 101, 181, 208-211, 227
Referring Domain Links, 101
Referring domains, 208-9
Region, 56, 120, 248
Registered, 81, 141, 206

Registrar, 142
Regulatory, 36
Reinforcing, 25, 107
Related, 12, 36, 40, 43-44, 46, 49-51, 56, 76-77, 84, 92, 94-95, 97-99, 102, 111, 126, 147-148, 150-151, 154, 157, 159, 171, 181-182, 186-187, 190, 193, 199-200, 202, 206, 208, 210, 216, 222, 230, 237
Relationship, 1, 4, 8, 14, 16, 33, 51, 61, 81, 84, 88, 94, 108, 121, 133, 146, 151, 176, 181, 184, 188, 192, 220, 224, 233-234, 236, 239
Release, 20-21, 30, 39, 54, 56, 61, 100, 102, 106, 109, 120, 136, 138, 142, 148-149, 151, 177, 183, 185-186, 193, 203-204, 206, 210, 214, 226, 230
Relevance, 71, 74, 76-78, 81-84, 86, 88-90, 94, 97-100, 108, 110, 116-117, 126, 141-143, 145, 147-148, 150-151, 155, 157-158, 161, 176, 181-182, 190-191, 200, 202, 205-209, 211, 213-216, 220-221, 224-225, 230, 232, 250
Relevance
   contextual, 98
   website's, 98
Relevance content, 143
Relevance score, 84, 99, 147, 150
Relevant, 50, 53, 56, 70, 72, 75, 78, 85, 87, 94, 98-99, 102-103, 111, 121, 126, 143, 147, 149, 152, 154-156, 158-159, 161-162, 171, 173, 176, 182, 190, 199, 202, 208, 220, 232, 237,
Religion, 38
Relocation, 186
Removal, 18, 23, 60, 104-105, 188
Removing content, 60
Renamed, 86
Reorganization, 186
Repair, 4, 13, 15, 18-19, 22, 26-27, 30, 42, 44, 46, 52, 57, 63-64, 66-67, 71, 120, 124, 128, 131, 134, 137, 243
Repeatable, 222
Repin, 217-218, 228
Report, 6, 25, 36-38, 45, 47, 55, 128, 137, 185, 245
Repository, 246
Represent, 48, 50, 80, 104, 127, 131-133, 139, 143, 170-171, 189, 212, 230
Repurposed, 177, 218
Reputation, 1, 4-23, 25-27, 29-35, 38-39, 41-52, 54-58, 60-68, 70-75, 78-80, 82-83, 85, 87, 89, 92, 94, 101, 105, 109, 111-112, 120-125, 127-128, 131-132, 135-140, 143-153, 155-156, 160-164, 166-167, 170-171, 175-177, 180-181, 190, 192, 195, 199-200, 205-206, 208-209, 212, 214, 217-219, 221-223, 225-226, 228-230, 232-234, 236-241, 243-244, 250
Reputation campaign, 125, 127-28, 131, 136, 138, 145, 147-48, 153, 155, 206, 212, 219, 228
Reputation campaign assets, 180, 195, 200
Reputation Campaign Monitoring, 229
Reputation control, 58, 65
Reputation Control & Search Engine Optimization, 63
Reputation damage, 51-52

S

272

CPSIA information can be obtained
at www.ICGtesting.com
Printed in the USA
LVOW01s0028300916

506808LV00008B/120/P